CONTENTS

The author (right) with his wife, Carol, sister in law Marylou and Brother Jack, after lunch at the Channelside restaurant n Clayton.

Dedication

To my wife, Carol, ever supportive and loving, without whom I would never have developed more than a halfhearted interest in restarting my desire to be an artist and writer.

To my old friend, mentor and colleague, Bill Galbreath. I owe him thanks for putting up with my whims as a set builder and designer, and teaching me about colors, mixing paint, and above all how to learn new things.

To Priscilla Marquez, who gave me a chance to perform again, both on and off stage, and who taught me patience, and many other things.

To all of those who have shown confidence in me and bought my books and paintings, and followed my work online.

Introduction

My office hutch. Looks messy, but it is not.

As I sit here in my "office," a computer hutch on one wall of my "studio," I am sorting the sketches I want to use for this book. I have been posting my art on three Facebook pages, "Clayton, NY Fans, Commercial" and "Art, it's what I'm at home with," my own Facebook page, and the group established as "Clayton, NY fans." The latter has grown to almost 1200 members, and people have been known to look in on the "commercial" page as well. I started drawing back in grade school, but the busy-ness of starting life as a college student put art on the back burner, other than drawing the occasional embarrassing cartoon (that's a separate story, which I'll leave for another time). A decade ago, I took it up again.

This is my second book about Clayton, the town in which I grew up and could not get out of fast enough as a teen. My friend Bryce Baker and I often discussed what we would do when we "got out." None of those adolescent dreams survived our leaving, but it does not matter. We each did things with our lives that made us happy in the long run. In my case it involved an eventual return to the place I wanted so badly to leave. In Bryce's case it was to travel, and become a professional angler for Bass Pro. I have been leaving and returning ever since the late 1960's, some six years after departing as a resident. Carol and I lived in Clayton for five summers, four of which we were gainfully employed.

Since then, we have retired, and returned nearly every year, renting for two to three weeks in July or August, trying not to look too much like tourists, blending in as much as possible. In that time, we both have taken hundreds of photos. Some I have used as subjects for paintings over the last decade since I took up pen, pencil and brushes again; and in that time, I decided to write, and began to submit articles to the area weekly newspaper, the Thousand Islands Sun. I wrote about my Clayton experiences, and sometimes about my art, most of which is Clayton, or 1000 Islands based. I find it difficult to get enthused about painting or writing something off that subject. I have done so, but it is more difficult. We have literally moved to artist's paradise, New Mexico, in the last year. I haven't found anything I want to paint, yet.

The artist/author at work in "the studio", in the same corner as the "office." This is a sketch of my old studio, in Georgia. The one in New Mexico is much the same, only bigger.

I got tired of trying to find storage for paintings that were not selling. While they do sell, the inventory took up too much space. I decided to go to watercolor on paper, and digital art, instead of acrylic on canvas. Just recently I started looking at my sketches that were made from photos in preparation, or study, for painting a scene. I should mention that I don't do people much, hence "scene." Sketching, and not going further with a watercolor painting, appealed to me. It is much faster, and satisfies my desire to relax using art. To my surprise, people seem to want to buy them more than the paintings. Of course, they don't command a large commission, but that is not why I am "doing art." I have been publishing them on-line and writing a little story about why I sketched them, or what they are. Several people have suggested I should put a book together. I thought that was a great idea, so some 100 new sketches later, here it is.

I have been neglecting my first love, writing for the Thousand Islands Sun. Writing articles has given me the opportunity to practice using Word and other writing tools, and during that time I made money (not much) writing freelance. I wrote four "Clean Romance" novellas for another author, and three were successes after publication. I should mention my various NDA's here (non-disclosure agreements). I can't reveal the titles.

My degree from Syracuse University is in English, (Edu) and I spent a great deal of time in the building in the following sketch. It is a digital drawing I did of the place where I first seriously studied writing and wrote my first (unpublished) novel pages under the direction of Mr Guereschi. I spent a lot of time in that building, and could almost draw it from memory, but this is from a photograph I took while visiting S.U. 38 years later in 2002. I love this building. The interior has been renovated to modern office space, but it's still the same old "HL."

After a missed summer in Clayton due to the pandemic, and last summer's long drive across this great country from New

Mexico and back, I had little new to write about for the Sun. I hope to be picking up that thread again after this year's visit, when I am sure there will have been plenty of events and reminders of subjects to fill a page or two.

I hope you enjoy the book. I am having fun (and will have had fun) writing it. It has kept me out of trouble, and given me the impetus to do both of the things I love, writing and painting.

CLAYTON BACK THEN

{"(The town of) Clayton was formed from Orleans and Lyme, April 27, 1833, and was named in honor of Hon. John M. Clayton, United States Senator from Delaware." (Town of Clayton History from Child's Gazetteer (1890) pp 366-379}

If you grew up here, you know these things, have seen many of these things, these places. I decided to draw my memories, from my photos, and put them together.

Clayton was established as a place where commerce, on arguably one of the world's biggest rivers, was easily conducted. Trade, farming, logging and the ship building industry were carried out in and from here. Local history, available at the 1000 Islands Museum at 312 James Street in Clayton will inform you of the many entrepreneurs from all over the country and the world who came here to make their mark and their fortune. Butchers, bakers, candlestick and barrel stave makers; mariners, shipwrights, loggers, railroad men, quarrymen dairy farmers, doctors and dentists; actors and musicians and retired soldiers from the Revolution came here. Many prospered, and their families prospered, and many of the old family names are still around. Some are preserved in street names, seen on this map, or a new one on Google. Be sure to stop in at the Museum, and look up Sharon Borquin, the curator.

The village was given various names since its start, but ended up as Clayton. It was established in 1872, when residents decided to add an additional layer of government to the Town of Clayton. This year, 2022, will be its Sesquicentennial Celebration. Long before that day people had been coming here because it has a river flowing past it. Before the European settlers showed up there were native Americans, Indians, as they became known by the settlers and their descendants. These people settled here to enjoy the fishing and hunting, and probably farming that was possible. When General Sullivan led his troops through what was to become New York State, the natives were farming. And he ordered his troops to burn the settlements and the fields. I doubt Sullivan and his men ever got this far north. Winter got in the way, and they turned back after "pacifying" the indigenes, who did not appreciate the favor, and as far as I know, they still don't.

Evidence of that occupancy exists in abundance on the larger Islands in the St. Lawrence and, as my friend Bryce Baker and I discovered as kids, on the land away from the river. We used to find arrow heads and potsherds when we dug just below the surface on his grandfather's land, finding evidence that a settlement existed there, including the blackened remains of fire pits.

Around the time of French settlement in this area, European people began coming here to exploit the resources of the surrounding land and the river. After the Revolution, more came, and towns like Cape Vincent, Dexter, Depauville, La Fargeville, and Alexandria Bay started growing from the existing forests. Those forests were timbered for the tall trees that became ship's masts and timbers, and buildings. Ships made here were built to ply the St. Lawrence and Lake Ontario; but there was also a thriving lumber export industry. Log rafts were built and floated down the St. Lawrence, the lumber to be shipped across the sea to Europe, as well as supplying building material here in the early days of the U.S. Those deep forests of tall trees are gone now, mostly replaced, after being cleared for now unoccupied farmland, by open fields and brushy areas. In time, as the land returns to its natural state where farms have disappeared, the forests may be back. As the dairy farms disappeared in the last 50 years, we have watched the natural evolution of grassland back through brush to forest.

As the town grew up around the shipping and timber business, more people came to work there. In later years, streets were laid out in plan, and land was sold as home lots, and business properties. I have a map which shows the town from an aerial perspective, long before there were planes from which to take photos. Houses and businesses were drawn as they were in the late 1800's and early 1900's, with streets labeled much as they are today. It has hung on one of our walls, no matter where we have lived, since my brother gave it to me a long time ago. It, and the satellite photo that also hangs on the wall, remind me of where I was formed as a person, just like all those before me and since in this town.

The map in the photo below is of Clayton as it was between 1890 and 1910. It shows a busy, bustling harbor, and a waterfront considerably different from today.

I have labeled it so you can pinpoint places mentioned in this narrative, and where the sketches of these places are in town. The body of water running under the railroad tracks (6) was filled in during the early part of the 20th Century, and the iron bridge over French Creek (3) which carried the road to Cape Vincent is now a causeway and bridge, with a good portion of the easternmost part, South of the bridge having been filled in the mid to late 20th Century.

The houses I grew up in are visible in the upper left corner, on Graves Street (1) and Beecher Street (2). You can see my best friends 'houses (Jim Marshall 4, and Bryce Baker, 5) and the village water supply standpipe (which was replaced in the 60's, I believe) right behind and beside Marshall's. The Opera House, 7, and all four churches (Baptist, 10; St. Mary's, 11; Methodist, 12; Episcopal, 13) can be clearly seen as well. All these structures are still in evidence today, except for the Standpipe. These locations were all important landmarks to me when I was growing up. They have not changed much in 80 years. I have marked them on the map, so that the reader can see where they are, should they care to see them in person. Driving around Clayton to find them and see them is something we do every time we are there, though I am sure it bores the heck out of Carol.

Two important buildings in Clayton history, and in my family history, are the public school buildings. One, the original Clayton school, is now gone, and stood at Merrick and Mary Streets. It was replaced by a new building in 1942 -43, when my father, Robert Charles, took over as principal. The building was nearly finished, and in 1944 was finished. Our family moved to Clayton shortly after. The new school building became Clayton Central School, K-12. It was built on what in the days the map was made, vacant land, not a block from our home at the time, #2.

Hand drawn aerial map of Clayton as it was at the turn of the 20th Century.

The next sketch is from an old postcard showing Clayton as it was in the time of that map, including the horse trough in the center of "Main Street," now Riverside Drive.

That horse trough and fountain were gone when I was a boy, replaced by a war memorial in the shape of a lighthouse, with the names of soldiers lost in war drawn upon its wooden walls by my art teacher, "Prof" James DeStefano. The power poles shown in the picture were a fixture in Clayton, the lines strung upon them always in sight, and visible in every photo I and thousands of others took on the streets of Clayton. Until last year. Now they are gone over the downtown district. Over the last three years or more, a major project buried the power and phone lines, making the downtown even prettier than before.

To me, Clayton will always be a town that keeps its past as visible as possible. You will see very few examples of modern architecture here, and even on the busiest days, there is a quiet about the town that makes me think of how it must have been then, before airplanes, and trains and swarms of cars and trucks came into the picture. I've lived in big cities, and I prefer Clayton, if only I could live there.

Clayton Co 1905

Downtown Clayton, Ca 1905, from TI Museum postcard

Speaking of trains, one of the things that made Clayton a bustling commercial center, aside from the industry and mercantile development between 1700 and 2022, were the carloads of tourists and summer/holiday guests arriving daily at the rail terminal. The station was right on the river, convenient to the docks, where people met boats that would take them to island resorts, or the homes of their wealthy friends. It was within walking distance of hotels in town. Now there is an attractive pavilion, constructed to resemble that long gone rail station. It is a place that still attracts tourists, whether they come by car or boat. Sometimes even a passenger liner or large yacht will show up at the docks on its way up or down the Great Lakes - St. Lawrence waterway, now known as the Seaway. That waterway is one of the largest and longest in the world, containing, it's said, 1/5 of the world's fresh water.

Where the river touches Clayton, the St. Lawrence Seaway channel is one of the widest points affording those who stand on the shore a prime view of passing ships. There is a view of both Great Lakes freighters and an international parade of ships from nearly everywhere, not to mention the awesome beauty of the river and its many moods. The Queen of England and Britain once passed by here in her yacht, Britannia, accompanied by President Eisenhower.

You can't see it anymore, but across the channel is the remains of one of the summer homes built in the 1000 Islands by some of the millionaires of the late 19th and early 20th centuries. All that remains of Calumet Castle is the six-story water tower, the windows at the top of which are brightly lit at night. I had the privilege of touring the island and climbing up in that tower in 2014 with the caretaker, Mike Strouse and some longtime friends from the Muggleton family. That was something I had wanted to do since I went there as a ten-year-old with my brother, Jim. Later as a high schooler I watched them knock the castle down with dynamite, while I sat in one of the old wood and concrete benches at street level above the park at the village dock, listening to "experts" explain how it would never work.

That same area, with the same wood benches (now replaced with sturdy plastic ones) is pictured in the sketch below, which also shows the bustling waterfront and docks at what is now called Rotary Park. Carol and I still spend hours in the summer, sitting there and watching the people, the boats and the ships that pass by on this great riverscape. To me, it's better than watching TV. I hope someday, if you already have not done so, you will sit here and enjoy one of the prettiest rivers in the world.

(Above) Rotary Park, with the old concrete and wood benches from back in the day.

Calumet Castle, as it was Ca. 1906. Acrylic Painting by the author from a postcard and memory

Calumet was never destined to become a tourist attraction, though it would have been a beauty. Vincent Dee and other investors were hopeful that it could be preserved as such, but boat tours to it never took off. It was, for a while, a boatel, where you could dock your boat and stay for a while. There is still some of that, with some of the dock space leased to self-contained stay aboard vessels, but the activity is not there anymore. The current owners use the island in the summer, and Mike Strause and his crew of expert groundskeepers tend to the island's beautiful gardens, as well as keeping up the build

ings and structures. The water tower has an apartment on the first floor, and some of the other buildings are very livable. The huge caretaker's house is well cared for, and occasionally occupied.

There are other living spaces as well. The Victorian home was moved to the island from Picton Island, which the builder and original owner also owned. He also owned the Frontenac Hotel on Round Island, just downriver from Clayton. It was a favorite destination while it existed, but it burned in 1911 and was never replaced. The post office that served island residents and the hotel is still functioning, but the hotel is long gone.

Calumet Water Tower. iPencil sketch by author.

Calumet Lagoon. iPencil sketch by author.

(above) Sunset over Calumet - iPencil sketch by author.

Base pencil sketch of the 16X20 acrylic painting of Calumet done from
Carolyn Vincent Bourgois 'postcard

Sketch of Frontenac Hotel on Round Island, from a post card of the time.

Frontenac Round Island Post Office, today. iPencil sketch from author's photo. This is a fully functioning post office, left over from the days the Hotel was here, approximately behind the clear area leading down to the waterfront.

Another large, imposing but not so magnificent structure was located in the footprint of today's Antique Boat Museum main building. It housed a major employer in Clayton right up until my high school years. I don't recall exactly when it was demolished, but it would have needed to go for the new museum building. I had friends whose mothers worked at the Hawn knitting mill. I knew nothing about it, other than, as the sign says, bathing suits and sweaters were made there. I can't recall the source or the accuracy of the information, but I seem to remember reading uniforms were made there during both wars. Don't quote me, but it sounds likely.

The Hawn Knitting Mill, or Clayton Manufacturing

This corner of Mary and Theresa Streets was an active manufacturing, boat building, and marine business site since the settlement of Clayton began in the 1700's. It was in sheltered French Creek Bay that log rafts were assembled to be floated up or down river to be used to make ships, homes, businesses and furniture somewhere else. Not all those logs went that route, however. First, early in the 19th Century, boat building became one of Clayton's biggest enterprises. The lagoon made by the slight extension of land on which the museum now sits was home to a thriving boat building industry. Another lagoon now defined by filled land between modern Merrick Street (then Merick, named after the owner of the shipyard until Capt. Johnston bought it in 1867), and John Street approximately where Rotary Park is now. The latter, I believe, was where Captain Johnston's shipyard was. Sailing ships of the two masted schooner variety were built then, and later, Capt. Johnston built steamboats that plied the river until the early 1900's. In the preceding map you can see steamboats doing just that on regular routes.

Because the river is a place of great, sometimes swift change in weather, and a large body of deep, cold water, accidents happen which are common only in maritime situations. The Great Lakes and the St. Lawrence are graveyards full of the result of those accidents. Many are, like the Edmond Fitzgerald, storied in nature. Not so storied are the mishaps that resulted in the loss of log rafts. The river bottom is laced with old logs, and I mean very old logs, which broke off those rafts and eventually sank. Local divers and salvors have "rescued" some of those deep-water casualties, and the sale of said logs, oak, walnut, maple, etc., can be quite lucrative. When we lived at French Creek Marina between 2004 and 2010, we used to walk by a stack of such logs, recovered by the Owner, Wilbert Wahl and his sons. A 400-year-old oak log is something to see. They were preserved by the fresh, cold water under high pressure at the bottom of the river, wherever they were found. Also visible around town and particularly at the Marina, are antique anchors recovered from where they became snagged at anchorage, or as a result of a sinking.

It is interesting to note that at some point, and I don't have the exact history here, the building you can see peering out from behind the Clayton Manufacturing building became Brooks Lumber yard, using at least one of the original buildings for millwork. You can see that building, which is used for display and boat building classes, at the Antique Boat Museum.

Boat livery at the Antique Boat Museum. You can
take out a St. Lawrence Skiff here

In the above iPencil sketch of the boat livery you can see
its position relative to French Creek Bay, with Bartlett Point

visible in the center background. It was no wonder that ship building was appropriate in this location. With a sheltered bay. And a lagoon available, there was plenty of room. The stone building that houses the boatbuilding exhibition is out of the frame to the right.

BROOKS-LUMBER

The above sketch is one I did for another project. It is based on a photo I took my Junior or senior year which was used in Brooks 'ad in the 1960 Calumet yearbook. Details are sketchy, pardon the pun, but you get the idea. I just sold a print of this one. There are sketches and there are sketches. Some are more detailed than others. Less sketchy, in other words. The docks behind Brooks Lumber were a favorite place for local swimmers. Particularly after the Clayton Beach, next door to the Knitting Mill, closed. I was very young then and paid little real attention to such things, but my understanding of it was that it was closed due to the polio epidemic at the time. Even after vaccines were distributed and successful, most people did not go back there to swim. The water was quite likely contaminated. It probably no longer is.

"Acrylic on 16X20 canvas, "Boat Slip" – as the slip might have looked in 1955.

Sketch of the boat slip from a later photo. On this
particular day it was quite empty, unlike 1955.

Just around the corner, past the private home of the Youngs
family, was a large marina operated by Tom Turgeon and his
family. My father kept his boat there in the 1950's. It was an 18'
Lyman Islander with a 45HP Gray Marine engine. Mom, Dad
and I spent a lot of time in the summer in that boat. He had a
16 'Lyman before that, which fit in a small, rented boathouse
on Steele's Point. But the water on that side of the point was
too shallow for the "new" boat. Dad bought the bigger Lyman
in 1954 and moved to Turgeon's. The slip looked nearly the
same in 2008 when I took the photo the painting below is
based on. His boat, Le Bouton Petit Argent, is purposely the
only boat in the slip. It was never this empty.

CLAYTON BOWLING ALLEY

Sketch from a photo of the author's approach style
at the Clayton Bowling Alley (Burr's)

Bryce and I bowled there in a school league, and often during open bowling. We set pins there as well, as a part of our learning experience, I guess. That is a dangerous job, if you're not careful. We got paid in bowling privileges and a very small wage. It is pretty hard work. The alleys were managed for the Burrs by Bernard Dine, who was effectively our boss, and a character. Bowling was the only sport I was ever good at. When the alleys were closed after Aubrey's Bowling Lanes opened in the late 50's on James Street, we were treated to automatic pin setters and ball returns. I once bowled a 299 there, but it went unrecorded in the records because it was open bowling, and Bryce was my only witness. Now I have not been able to bowl at all since my fifties exposed a disc problem in my back. The next sketches illustrate Clayton as I saw it as a boy, later as a young man, and still later as an adult. The photos all cover places that were and are no longer. The buildings may still be there, but their occupancy has changed. When they are not there, usually the cause was fire, often very serious fire which effectively took the building out of service entirely or made it impractical to rebuild. Almost as often it was economic circumstances, sometimes when the founding family aged out of the business and the children were not interested in running it. That has been the case with many of the dairy farms that dotted upstate New York when I was a boy. They are now overgrown fields. Some of the buildings that remained have been repurposed, especially if they were sound and in a good location. I will show a few of those here.

First is Cantwell's Creamery. In the next chapter you will see it as "The Koffee Kove," a thriving restaurant in the same location. We got our milk deliveries and occasionally groceries from Cantwell's. The drawing includes Frank Cantwell, and since I am really bad at drawing people other than in caricature, it does not look much like Mr. Cantwell. But he was in the photo it was sketched from, so I included him.

A very bad sketch of Farnk Cantwell in front of his
store, from the artist's 1959 photo

At some point, Byrne Dairy and other large corporate dairies edged out stores like his, but as far as I recall he was still running it when I left in 1960. I paid little attention to the store after that, as I was rarely in Clayton, and preoccupied with other things during my college and early marriage years.

This hurried sketch is of Hungerford Hardware,
from a photo I took around 2002

The Eagle Shoppe, Ink Sketch from author's photo

I was quite fond of Hungerford Hardware, and used to buy things there, for me or my dad, out of the bins of nails, screws, nuts and bolts – and other hardware items that were just fun to shop for here. When Carol and I moved to Elmira there were several neighborhood hardware stores. But when Ace and True Value showed up, they went out of business. There was one in Horseheads, north of Elmira, which reminded me of Hungerford's, but it too went away with the modern chain hardware business plan. To this day I am delighted when I find a real hardware store somewhere, and I go out of my way to patronize it occasionally. They have stuff you can't find at Home Depot.The above sketch of the Eagle Shoppe shows a going concern, with a presence in Clayton and even a Web site – eagleshoppe.com. The reason for the inclusion of this sketch is one of the location's former tenants. When I was fourteen, I worked as a busboy at McCormick 'Restaurant, a venue which does not exist anymore, and is featured in the next chapter on restaurants. But being a bus boy during the school year only provided weekend work, so I was fortunate enough to get daily work as a news carrier. The pay was peanuts, but the tips could be good, and you only had to work two hours or so a day, six days a week. I started as a sub, and never did get my own route, delivering for the Watertown Daily times and the Saturday Post Standard out of Syracuse. Sometimes I'd do a Sunday sub for the Post Standard. I worked almost all of the routes in town as a sub.

My friends Paul Carpenter, Jim Marshall, Fran Gray and Bryce Baker also delivered; with a few other older guys I did not know so well. The papers came to Clayton by bus, which arrived around 3:30 to 4 every day from Syracuse via Watertown. Merle Dailey's smoke shop and shoeshine parlor were in this building, and it was also a place to buy bus tickets. There was another bus station in town, but this was where the bus stopped in the 50's to drop off papers. When I was in my freshman year at S.U. I took the Greyhound bus out of

Syracuse, and it came through Watertown to Clayton at the same time every weekday.

Harry's, later the Driftwood, sketch from TI Museum post card

I have a photo of Paul and Jim in front of Daly's in 1959, the last year I delivered. My Senior year, 1960, was too busy for papers. Unfortunately, since I don't do people well, I never did a sketch of that. The street and the building are not much changed at that location, and if you were to go back in time, you'd still recognize it. That is one thing I love about Clayton, which I am not sure is shared by many. Things on the street do not change much, only the players.

The view from the back of the Driftwood in 1958, from author's photo.
Including a coal fired ship. iPhone sketch from author's 1955 photo

This business was a favorite for many years, even after it changed hands. It was still there for a few years after I left. I remember it was there in 1965 when Carol and I visited Clayton, not long after our marriage. In the mid 50's it became the Driftwood and was typical of this sort of 50's place. So typical was it that I ghostwrote a novella around a setting very much like it years later for someone else. My NDA says I can't tell you more than that, other than that the book sold better than any of my own have.

When you walked in the door you immediately saw a couple of horseshoe shaped counters with round-top spinning seats bolted to the floor. Straight out of an Archie Cartoon. I loved it and spent far too much time and money in there out of my paper boy work. Great coffee and great milkshakes, the latter thick, but not like the kind you can get a hernia from trying to suck up through your straw, and not too thin, like there was no ice cream in it. I remained addicted to that format until my late 60's, when I developed lactose intolerance – no more milkshakes. I'd have to describe it to waitresses like that to get it anywhere else usually, much to their amusement.

There was a back room, open to the front, with windows facing the river and the coal dock. This sketch, done on an iPhone, is based on a photo I took out this window in 1957 or 1958. I always like the photo because it features not only the river view, but the coal fired laker tied up, refueling, at the coal dock that is now Frink Park pier.

Later in life, a few years ago, I ghostwrote four Romance novels, using my memories of the Driftwood. Three actually sold.

Wood and Concrete benches at what is now Rotary Park.
Grayscale photo of painting from author's photo

It was a foggy morning when I shot the photo this 16X20 acrylic on canvas painting is drawn from. We used to come here and sit after getting a cone or a milkshake somewhere, or just sit and watch the world go by. Carol and I still do this. The benches are plastic now, but not much else has changed.

The photos for the last two sketches of the TI Inn were both taken before it closed. We last ate there in 2004 with Carol's aunt Dorotha and cousins Sue and David. We went to visit the Coast Guard cutter at the dock that is now Frink Park. This is right across the street, and the photo for the first sketch was taken from the park, pre- pavilion.

The sign has always fascinated me, in the sense that I've marveled at how much information they got on it. This hotel was one of the places that perennially gets credited with the invention of Thousand Island Dressing by the wife of a local guide who worked there. Since all the people involved are no longer here to set us straight, it will forever remain a legend.

The sign lists fishing guides, wreck dives and dive lessons, food, and other things. I never saw it as a garish advertising example. Maybe that's just me, because you can't say the sign was tasteful, but it did what it needed to: stood out without being annoying, and to me, it became a landmark. It's gone now, discarded and lying out back where trash was placed when the Inn was open. I have often wished it, as well as the hotel, could be preserved. We'll see. The next few years may work out that way.

(above) Streets Insurance Agency in 1959

The last I knew the building below is occupied by the Chamber of Commerce. When I was a lad Mr. Streets was one of my Father's friends, and sort of his boss as a member of the School Board. He admired Mr. Streets, and I believe Dad learned what he knew of the river from the fishing trips he took with him. I knew two other insurance agents in town, or at least their children, but this was likely the first insurance agency I ever set foot in, and to this day, when I think "insurance office," this is what comes to mind. I had a thirty-year career in insurance, starting as an adjuster, then an agent, and finally combining the latter with a position in the business department at Elmira College teaching insurance to people who wanted either more business credits or a New York State certificate to take the Agents or Brokers license test. I spent years in many insurance offices and my own, but this building is the prototype my mind pops up when I think "office." I took this photo for an ad for the agency in the 1960 Calumet Yearbook.

The other "pickle." The parking area in front of McCormick's Restaurant in the late 50's or early 1960's. (Greyscale photo of my watercolor painting)

At the other end of Riverside Drive (Water Street in the early days of the 20th Century) there is a metered parking area with head in diagonal parking which has been there for as long as I can remember. It has been preserved and is now much more attractive than it was then. For one thing all the overhead power lines and tall poles are gone. On the left side of the painting, you can just see the alley between McCormick's and the boat line pavilion, and Waldron's Jewelry store right next door to the latter. You can also see the then still standing Ellis block just beyond Waldron's. These are now Bella's and "Forever Park" respectively. On the right you can see Kennedy Drugs in the center background, and all the way down the street in the center you can see the building that used to be Nunn's Appliances and is now Rak's variety and clothing store. Right behind Nunn's/Rak's would have been the building the Driftwood occupied. In the far background you can see Washington Island, which was later developed after Gerald Ingerson built a causeway and a bridge to it. It looks considerably different now, with properties approaching a million dollars in value.

Notice the variety of cars parked in the Pickle. I learned to drive a standard shift in my brother's 1951 Plymouth and got my license in 1958. I think one of those cars is of that vintage. The name for this area is not really "the Pickle." That was the area in the center of Riverside farther down, in front of all the stores on the North and South sides of the street. But I've been told that some people refer to the parking area as "The Pickle." Either way, I use this photo as an example of how little Clayton has changed visually over the last 100 years. By 1922 the era of conflagrations was over. We had and still have a terrific fire department that kept that from happening, and an ordinance that no frame buildings could be constructed in the downtown area, ever again. So other than the removals of the power lines, the cosmetic changes to the street and sidewalks and the removal of the Pickle, the lighthouse and the horse trough, Clayton looks a lot like it did in 1920. I hope it stays that way. USA Today listed Clayton as one of the top ten small towns in the country last year, and this year it seems to be still on top. If you've never been here, you've missed something unique, magical and lovable.

Pulver's Store, now Michael Ringer's Art Gallery

This corner building was severely damaged by fire in the early 1900s. All of the buildings in the block except this one and the Johnston house were completely destroyed. When this building was rebuilt the third story was added. An interesting feature is the addition of gargoyles at each corner. When I was a lad, this was Pulver's Department Store, modeled after Woolworth stores. I spent a lot of time in there, just walking up and down aisles, wishing I could afford a new Army Man, or a "Clayton" souvenir tin whistle, and other trinkets. We bought our replacement Christmas bulbs and ornaments here. For a while Kennedy Pharmacy occupied part of the building, until they closed after the new chain drug store opened. Now it houses Michael Ringer's Clayton Art Gallery. I think I enjoy walking those aisles as an adult artist as much as I did as a child.

Hubbard House, from photo courtesy of the 1000
Islands Museum postcard collection

My oldest brothers Jack and Jim worked at the Hubbard House as bellhops and errand boys. Whenever I think of bellhops, I picture Johnny Roventini and hear "Call for Phillip Morris." Jack and Jim didn't wear uniforms like that. The hotel was a three-story building that survived as a third iteration after several conflagrations, one of which destroyed most of downtown long before I was born.

In the sketch below you can see, left to right, River Rat Cheese,, the Porch and Paddle store, and Gray's Flower shop. The latter has now been replaced by River Yoga. Where the Yoga studio is now, and Gray's Flowers before it, was Graves' Pharmacy. For decades it was the place where my family got their prescriptions. I have no idea why it was there and not Ellis Drugs, but I recall having to pick up prescriptions for my mother, and before that, waiting for her to pick up prescriptions for me or the rest of the family.

McKinley Block, where Graves Drugs was housing River
Rat Cheese, Gray's Flowers (now River Yoga)

I had a lot of prescriptions even back then, as a sickly child with asthma and hay fever and frequent bouts of bronchitis. While waiting I would peruse the comic book rack, occasionally being told "those are for sale, you know" by the clerk behind the antique marble soda bar that had rotating stools and back bar mirrors. Occasionally I would look across the street to the Hubbard House and see older tourists sitting in the rockers on the verandah. And now I am an older tourist.

Crandall's GLF feed store from photo courtesy Thousand
Islands Museum postcard collection

At the top of the James Street hill, past the lighted 1000 Islands
sign, is the light at "Gay Head Corners," the local name for
the State and James crossroads, with the only traffic light in
town, then. On the Southwest corner was Bogenshutz's Gay
Head Market. My mother loved the ground round she could
get there. It was just lean enough to suit, and she could send
me on my bike to get it every week. Sometimes she would
call in advance, sometimes I would end up waiting for it. You
can see the back corner of the store, with the Bogenshutz's
apartment above it This store remained in operation for many
years after I left. When Mr. Bogenshutz passed away and his
widow, Marjorie, sold the store and the building to Bert and
Rae Patterson, who ran it for many years. South of the market
was Frank (Cy) Crandall's GLF feed store. Mr. Crandall bought
the feed store after World War II and ran it until the 1960's,
selling out to Agway. The building was remodeled many years
later as Christiansen Realty.

West on State Street from James was Bernie Consaul's market. My friend Bryce Baker used to work there when we were in High School. I don't have a photo to do a sketch from, and the market is now a tax preparation office that barely resembles Consaul's. The store remained open until around 2009. When we lived at the French Creek Marina, we used to go there for milk, bread, the Watertown Daily Times and the Sunday Post Standard. I can't recall the exact date it went out of business. There was another little store on Reese Street, just around the corner from Theresa Street, but I don't remember it being open when I delivered papers there. It is now a private residence.

The sketch above shows the front of Bogenshutz'z Gay Head Market, done from a photo courtesy of the Thousand Islands Museum post card collection.

Drive Northeast on State and a left at John St., Just past the Shurfine store takes you to Union Street. Turn right on Union and go East to Merrick. At the corner of Merrick and Union you will see the building in the sketch below. It is an apartment building now, but back then it was Fink's Grocery Store, where if you had $.09 you could get a large single cone of the ice cream of the day, and a penny back from your dime. It was like dozens of small country stores I have been in since. They seemed to have a little bit of everything. I wish they still existed, but the big box business model put them out of business long before Walmart. Their daughter, Linda, was a year behind me in high school, and we used to hang out together occasionally. Date would be too strong a word. We were friends. RIP Linda.

In the other direction, south on Merrick Street (it is one way now, so you cant go north from State) to State Street is the Shurfine Supermarket, which used to be a Big M. When I was in school that spot and the lot the bank next door is on was occupied by Gray's cottages. I used to "help" Fran mow the lawn there. I wasn't much help due to severe grass allergy, but we hung out afterward. A little west of there was Potter's store, which later became the present liquor and wine store, and Bombard's bar and grill, I used to go to Potters to get milk at $.05 a quart. Mom would let me get a Clark bar with change from the dime she gave me. My friend Fran Gray's father established the wholesale food, tobacco, and candy warehouse behind Potter's.

Fink's store, from a Google Street View screen shot.

There also used to be a small one-story block building housing a plastic extrusion and molding factory. I worked there for Norm Wagner my Senior year summer after I got fired from McCormick's for reading a book on the job. Learned a real lesson there. If you're at work, be working. That's your job.

PRE BELLA'S

Uncle Sam Tours and gift shop, ca 2003. Ink Sketch from author's photo.

In the restaurants chapter that follows it is mentioned that Carol worked in the boat line terminal and gift shop in the building that used to be Waldron Jewelry and is now Bella's. Above is the sketch I made of it a few years back, which includes the blank space to the right whichwhich was torn down to make way for Gray's Wholesale. is now "Forever Park." The reference photo for the sketch was taken in 2004, when she worked there. The sketch is of the rail station in Clayton as it would have looked back in the days of steam trains and ferries. The marks from the rail bed you see just to the right of center at the bottom of the sketch can still be seen in the granite bedrock of Frink Park.

Sketch from a post card, courtesy of the 1000 Islands
Museum from their postcard collection

Today, the shipyards, the coaling station, most of the hotels, and many of the old support businesses of this time are gone. But you are looking at what really put this town on the map. "Tourists" from far and wide came to see what they had been told was a paradise, with "good air" and healthy living. I doubt they came here in the winter much, but spring summer and fall they came in droves. They boarded the steamboats you can see at the dock and dispersed to the castles, luxurious Victorian homes and hotels scattered around the islands mostly downriver from Clayton. They also stayed at the local, land-side hotels like the Cassidy (Riverview), O'Brian's, the Herald House, and The Hubbard Hotel. From all of these they could find, as on the sign for the 1000 Islands Inn (formerly the Herald House) says, fishing guides and island tours, shore dinner parties, dancing at the Clayton Casino, shows at the Opera House and more. In my teens Clayton was still a tourist mecca, with little real industry in addition to that, except for Frink Snowplow, Hawn garment factory, Stabler and Baker,

GM Skinner fishing lures, a cheese factory, and the marine business of maintaining boats. The trains were gone, but people still came, now by bus and car. There used to be many places with "rooms to let," and small motels and cottages. Those are mostly gone now, but there are B&B's, such as the one a block south of Riverside Drive, across from the post office. It is called the McKinley House, after the prominent Clayton ship builder at the time who also built the McKinley block previously illustrated. This B&B is a reasonably priced venue for family events and short or long stays. We know the hosts, and believe me it's great. You need reservations, of course. This house was the Blake Residence when I lived here as a boy, then a young man, then as an apartment house. It has been continuously occupied since it was built by Mr. McKinley.

I have barely touched on the history of Clayton. For a closer study, should you wish to know more about the area, its people and their ancestors, you really need to stop in and check out the exhibits, library, and the extensive photo collection and family histories at the Thousand Islands Musuem. Anyone can help you, but you should ask for Sharon Bourquin. She has extensive knowledge of Clayton, and may direct you to the info you are looking for, or I'm sure, assign someone to help you.

Today Clayton is busier than ever. People seem to flock to other places, but many come back to Clayton, year after year, just as we do. There is something magical about the place, charming maybe, as opposed to frenetic, as some resort areas have become. It's a good place to relax, enjoy the scenery and the beauty of one of the world's greatest rivers. And if you love boats of all kinds, this is the place to be, to see them, new and old.

PARKS

I was once told there are too few places in Clayton to sit along the river that are not expensive, i.e. not restaurants and coffee shops. I remember thinking that the comment was made by someone who had not spent much time in Clayton. This is a town with more parks, eleven if you count the Mary St. Town Dock, than most towns its size. Four of them are riverside parks, with great views, and plenty of benches. Should your desire be to sit beside the river and have a snack and a beverage (nonalcoholic), all of them are free, and you can easily find a seat, or bring your own.

I'll start with the one closest to Lake Ontario, and work downriver. Centennial Park is sited on the space once occupied by a parking lot that served both the American Boat Line and McCormick's Restaurant. It is beautifully landscaped, with a long seawall river walk, benches, flowerbeds, and a gazebo. It overlooks Bartlett Point, the seaway channel, Wolfe, Carlton, Grindstone, Governor's and Calumet Islands, and a constant stream of boat traffic - both large and small. The painting below was a commission for Brenda (Cummings) Dix. It is a rendering of her parents seated at a bench in Centennial park gazing at the river they loved, and Grindstone Island. The white barn roof in the distance is the farm they ran until they retired.

The boats represent ones you could expect to see from this spot, a Canada Steamship Lines laker, a small sailboat and a Lyman Islander headed out to fish. Most of the benches on the waterfront like this have a plaque dedicating the bench to well known Clayton residents. It's a great place, uncrowded, to sit and watch the river. I'm convinced that the Cummings often sit in this spot, in spirit. I was very pleased when it was done, as quite often you can see a ship, and sometimes two, passing up or down bound. It is often the first thing we see when we get to Clayton and make our first drive "downtown." It is only one of five places in town where you are greeted by this sight as you drive toward the river, or along Riverside drive.

The Cummings Bench at Centennial Park

I did this St. Mary's painting for a friend, based on a photo I took in front of St Mary's Church on James, near the top of the hill. In the lower left corner you can see blue sky and river between the trees in the distance. In reality the gap is smaller than the painting shows, but I wanted it in there. That space's designation as a "forever" open place happened after I painted it. I hope it stays that way.

St Mary's Church looking down James toward "Forever Park.".
You can almost see the park at the end of James Street, lower left

That space is the next park, located about a block down river from Centennial Park. I can't recall its actual name, or if it even has one, so I refer to it as "Forever Park". There are no structures or benches here, and there will probably never be. I say probably because never is a very long time. But the village has so designated this strip of land, donated to it in perpetuity with the stipulation that it never be developed, or be built upon.

The park itself is simply that open space, with an "S" curve sidewalk leading to the riverside. You can see Calumet Island and the water tower in the center on the skyline. This space opened up when the Ellis block, housing apartments and Ellis Drugs, burned and was torn down. It remained just a grassy vacant lot, an open space for anyone to walk through to the river, for several decades. The owners refused to sell it, as it was their desire for it to remain open. In its heyday, the Ellis store was nearly, if not actually, a landmark. There was the drugstore part, and a news and sundries section, with souvenirs of the Thousand Islands for sale, as well as boat line tickets.

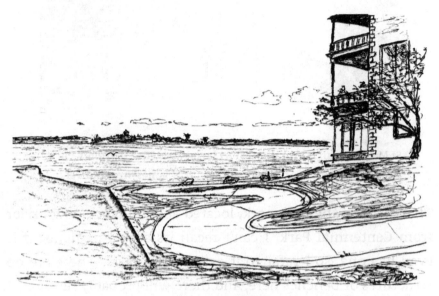

The winding path leading down the hill to the River Walk.

The Clayton Boat Line sold tickets next door in a pavilion, and in good weather you could wait there for one of the boats, or in the enclosed, glassed-in porch at the back of the Ellis store. My biggest thrill as a pre-teen was to spend part of my allowance on the latest Marvel comics for sale in the Sundries and Magazine section. I used to save the good ones, in a box in the back "attic" room of the house we lived in on Beecher Street. When we moved to the "new" house on Graves, my mother threw the box away. Imagine the value of those comic books today.

Memorial Park lighthouse and Calumet Island. Ink sketch from author's photo

Another block walk down river on Riverside Drive takes you to Memorial Park, where stands a newer, masonry lighthouse that incorporated and replaced the wooden one which used to sit at the East end of "the Pickle," a median strip that separated east and west lanes of Riverside Drive. overflow parking. It was called the picle for its oval shape. The median it formed was removed around1955.

The new lighthouse memorial and flagpole are on a level, railed platform fronted by paving blocks with names of war veterans who died serving their country. Behind the red granite light house, raised above the curved dock access road, is a level area built with blocks of the local red granite, with benches and cannons pointed at Calumet Island and the Sea Way Channel, in case of invasion. I'm kidding on that last statement. The story was that Mr. Emory, who owned Calumet, donated money to have the little park built to placate his wife, who wasn't happy with the back of the buildings facing the river. Not my story, just what I was told. We used to ride those cannons as kids, as if they were horses. No one ever stopped us, and we never did any damage to them. The view here is a little restricted by the buildings on each side. In my childhood the one on the left was Hungerford Hardware, where I learned to love wandering around in hardware stores. It is now a Christmas Store. The one on the right was a tourist gift and craft shop and is now the offices of Thousand Islands Land Trust (TILT). The lighthouse like water tower is visible on Calumet Island on the skyline

The painting of Calumet Castle is one I did from a Post Card provided to me by my friend, Carolyn Vincent Bourgeois, showing the "summer home" of millionaire Tobacco giant Charles G. Emery. It was sold in the early 1950's by the Emery family, and after a fire in the summer of 1956, the castle was razed - dynamited actually - and only the outbuildings remained, including a very large Victorian caretaker's house that was actually moved there across the ice from Picton Island, before the castle was built.

When we could find any that were flat enough, my best friend Bryce Baker and I used to skip stones from the heavy wooden dock at the edge of the shore, where the river walk is now. We often sat in the benches and wondered what kind of ship would come along next, watched the island mail boat unload when it came in, or just people watched. The latter is still one of my favorites. During that period traffic on the river changed. Lakers were converted from coal to oil to diesel. In the late 1950's, with the advent of the St. Lawrence Seaway, it changed again. Now we saw, and still see, ships from all over the world join the already busy river traffic. One of the features of our Class of 1960 Calumet Yearbook was a number of ship photos, including a heavy cruiser and large cargo vessels, with the highlight being a front and back cover photo of Queen Elizabeth's yacht Britannia, which came up the Seaway in celebration of the waterway's opening. President Eisenhower accompanied her aboard for a time.

As we got older, we didn't sit there as often. We moved down Riverside Drive to what was, as far as I knew then, a nameless park at the village docks. If memory serves, there were girls involved, though they mostly paid attention to Bryce. He was quite tall for his age, around 6', and towered above my 5'4". Many of the boats that came in brought families, and a few young ladies our age, from Round Island, down river.

What later became Rotary Park was always a gathering place for both young and old. In the painting you can see Reinman's department store, which was then a cigar store, at the corner of John and Riverside Drive. It was behind us as we sat in one of the old wood and concrete benches. Those benches, repainted and repaired every year, provided seating for locals and tourists alike. They were at street level above a green space with two large trees separated by a sidewalk that led from the docks to stairs up to the street. For the last 10 years, just down the street from Reinman's I have set up an easel and a chair in front of The Scoop, one of the places to eat mentioned in later chapters. It has always been a treat that the Proprietor, Mary Zavistoski, has allowed me to take up that space. I can people watch and gaze across the street at the river of my youth and paint pictures of it. The Scoop now sits where Gonseth's bicycle and auto shop used to be.

In the grayscale print above of a16X20 acrylic on canvas of Rotary park from a floating dock (reference photo by author), Reinman's can be seen across the street, behind the corner of the Golden Anchor. The photo was taken in 2002. The Scoop is now in the part of the building in the Center that used to be occupied by Gonseth's.

On any given night in summer there was always traffic, both on Riverside drive and to and from the floating docks in front of the park. People would come in from the islands, day and night, to replenish groceries, to simply do errands or stroll around in Clayton or often, to have dinner in one of the restaurants. Nothing about that has changed, except the structure of the docks, the height of the trees, the addition of a lovely River Walk, and the occupancy of the buildings.

Once there was a building housing a locker plant, another for the telephone office, where female operators handled local phone traffic on a PBX system, and the customs office. Now in that space there is a building renovated by the local Rotary Club, with a flat observation deck on top, and a dock master's office, and public bathrooms on the ground/riverside level. Attilio's pizza and Italian restaurant, a massage and health salon (now a popcorn store) are sandwiched in between the new building on the west end and offices and an art studio on the east end. Attilio's has a nice, covered deck overlooking the park docks and the river. Go there if you're in Clayton. Beer, pizza and a great view.

On the West end of the park was the Golden Anchor. Except for a 10-year hiatus, there has been a restaurant in this spot since the 1890's, under different names.

The spa and Attilio's, ca 2009.

It served meals to hungry tourists, locals and boat crews for decades. Sitting on the benches at street level, it was possible to see the activity inside. Waitresses scurried to take orders and deliver food. It was still popular after a long history as a restaurant catering both to locals and to the many summer visitors, until, in the beginning of the Millennium, it wasn't. For whatever reasons it closed in the early part of this century. The drawing is based on my photo taken in 2002, not long after it had closed for good. It was torn down a few years later, leaving an open wound in the waterfront next to the park. It was replaced by a beautiful new building with apartments on the top floors, Di Prinzio's Market and Freighters variety store on the first floor, and a full service Di Prinzio's restaurant at river level on the side facing Calumet Island. There is a riverside patio, with one of the best views in town at river level facing the ship channel and Calumet.

The floating Village Docks at Rotary Park have changed little and are carefully maintained. On a busy day the traffic to and from these docks is nearly constant, under the watchful supervision of one or two dock masters. There are now Adirondack chairs at river level, where sunsets can be enjoyed in comfort. One of our favorite things is watching how people land and disembark. After years of boat watching, we can easily tell who knows what they are doing and those who only think they do. You can spot a "River Rat" right away. They are expert at landing, even on a rough day, and the ease is a joy to watch. The other sort can be skilled as well, but the novices have provided us with quiet, private laughs as they try to dock without damaging pier or hull or having someone fall overboard. We've seen that happen, and we try not to make too much of it. You can ruin someone's day by laughing at them, and their day has already been made miserable enough. People watching is a sport, entertainment, but there is no need to be rude.

The Golden Anchor in 2002. Ink sketch from author's photo

In the following photo the figures in the center at street level are the people with whom we often sat by the river. We discussed nearly everything we could think of, with few serious disagreements. The photo this was based on was shot from the Clayton Island Tours boats as it departed for a sunset cruise in 2010. Carol and I and Chris and Lue Muggleton were on it with the rest of the folks from our class of 1960, Clayton Central School Reunion, held at O'Brien's Restaurant that year. We all waved as we departed.

Digital painting, "The Bench O'Knowledge" at Rotary Park

You'll see a lot of gulls when you visit, and they can appear very friendly. Gulls are hungry nearly all the time. Please don't feed them as, though fun, it can be dangerous or at least very scary if you attract a large flock.

There are two ways to get to the next park, the "new" Riverwalk at river level from RotaryPark, behind the buildings on Riverside drive, or the street level.

Take the River Walk down river to the next Park. The empty space behind the buildings housed a coaling station and coal storage building which burned for a week in 1956.

The monochrome painting pictured below was done from my photo, one of the first of many I took with my new Kodak Brownie Hawkeye.

There is no trace of the coal terminal, except for the deep grooves in the bedrock, visible as you walk the street level

Curious Seagull. Ink Sketch from author's photo

into the next and last riverside park. These grooves are left over from the railroad sidings that led to the coal tipple. Coal cars were lined up by an old steam yard engine, which used to sit idling in the yard when I was a little boy. I was afraid of it, but my dad took me near, to see that it was just a machine. Coal fired trains were phased out of service in the late 40's, replaced, like the river steamers, by Diesels. I once had a model railroad aficionado at a model train show tell me I was far too young to remember what a steam train whistle sounded like He was selling wood whistles that did indeed sound like one. No, I'm not.

Pencil Digital painting of Rotary Park Village docks, with the Golden Anchor in the center left, and TILT headquarters to the right

Seventy years ago, I used to love hearing them, as I lay in bed at night in the house on Beecher Street, when they crossed the East Line Road on the way in or out of town. When the new diesels came in they had to add horns, so people could hear them approaching the crossing. My dad worried about school buses getting hit by a train.

The action in Clayton for many years, was centered around the Railroad station, an old Victorian wooden passenger terminal which used to be the end or beginning of the trip to or from Clayton for the thousands of tourists the train brought. Until it didn't anymore. The current pavilion structure at Frink Park, as this park is known, sits in approximation of the spot the original terminal.

The action in Clayton for many years, was centered around the Railroad station, an old Victorian wooden passenger terminal which used to be the end or beginning of the trip to or from Clayton for the thousands of tourists the train brought. Until it didn't anymore. The current pavilion structure at Frink Park, as this park is known, sits in approximation of the spot the original terminal occupied. It offers a magnificent view of this section of the river and the Seaway channel from the foot of Wolfe Island all the way to the Thousand Islands Bridge, the lights of which you can see at night from here. There is no better view of the comings and goings of river traffic in the Village of Clayton, unless it is from the upper floors of the nearby Harbor Inn Hotel. The sunsets are magnificent, as they are also for the other parks, but the vista here is nearly 180 degrees.

The park is named after Carl Frink, who is known for inventing the V shaped plow that carried, and still carries, his name. The Frink factory stood in the spot where the Thousand Islands Harbor Hotel stands. There also used to be a hotel, The Riverview, (Cassidy's) in approximately the same spot, which was torn down for Frink's offices. Until the new hotel was built the large open area, a Federal Hazardous Waste cleanup site after the factory was razed, stood as an empty greensward with a great view of the river until the new hotel replaced it.

Since the covered pavilion including lights, sound system and heavy plastic benches was built, we have mostly transferred our seating preference to Frink Park. There is also a colorful line of heavy, comfortable plastic Adirondack Chairs, or you can bring your own. As mentioned previously, many large boats used to dock here to get fuel, either oil or coal. Some large liners still dock here on occasion, as well as large yachts. The water is not very deep here, and docking requires a relatively shallow draft. Or that you are a fish.

When I was a child, my dad caught a near record sized Great Northern Pike off the original heavy wooden timbered dock, while I played among the huge piles of coal to the Northeast, about where the front yard of the Thousand Islands Resort is. Just South of those coal piles was Frink Snowplow. The sign for the park is accompanied by a huge anchor recovered from the St. Lawrence and is visible as you drive toward the river and the park on Webb Street. The Frink Snowplow plant, which used to employ many Clayton residents, sat appropriately where the Hotel is now. There is a replica Frink V plow attached to the sign.

Typical Frink Park sunset

The lot was scrubbed of industrial wastes first and remained vacant for some years until this magnificent hotel was built. Coincidentally The hotel also stands partially on a spot once occupied by the Riverview Hotel/Hotel Cassidy back in the day. When I was 14 and delivering papers, it and O'Brien's were on my route. I delivered to the bar of each, as well as the Herald House, later the Thousand Islands Inn. All these hotels were close to the rail terminal serving commercial travelers as well as tourists. The only one still operational is O'Brien's, and they don't rent rooms now.

The new entrance to Frink Park. Large iron anchor would
be to the right. The yacht Freedom is visible behind the pavilion

The next sketches show the park as it was before the Pavilion
was added, with benches at the top and rows of wooden
bleacher like seating facing the water, as in the first two photos
below. The third photo is of a memorial, working life preserver,
meant to be used for someone in trouble in the water off the
dock. The dock is a concrete structure, complete with large
bollards to tie up the occasional larger craft, such as the one in
the digital painting of the cruise yacht Freedom, and the two
masted schooner in the sunset. Lots to see here, including the
view downriver all the way to the Thousand Islands Bridge,
often accompanied by a summer rainstorm. And finally, the
way the park looks today, with a new sign, the pavilion, and the
huge iron anchor kids still love to climb on. The concrete was
broken up by a huge excavator and replaced with walkways
with red brick trim.Many nights you will see fishermen and
women hoping to repeat my dad's catch of a large bass or pike

off the edge of the dock, when no ships are in port.

Benches at the top were our favorite place until the pavilion was built

The old seating plan

Memorial life preserver at railing in original park layout

View from the Pavillion looking Northeast at a typical summer shower.
Grayscale photo of acrylic painting from photo by author

One year I set up shop in the new (then) pavilion, hoping people would see me painting and decide to buy one. They didn't. I have always done my art because I enjoyed it, not because I wanted to be a rich artist. It's working.

Digital iPencil on iPad painting of display of author'spaintings at Frink Park

Two masted schooner, the painting on author's
easel in the above digital drawing

Just before sunset, from the pavilion

Yacht Freedom, digital iPencil on iPad painting from author's photo

Digital Painting of Frink Park Pavilion. The modern building
in the background replaced the Golden Anchor.

Drive up Webb Street from Frink park and you will experience
the overarching effect of the older trees you miss on Riverside
Drive. The downtown trees will catch up, as they are all fast
growing species. This is one of my favorite drives, recalling
many sights from my youth. Too many to list here.

On the left side of Webb Street you will see fenced multi use
Lions park. Summers it is baseball and soccer, Fall is football,
and Winter it is flooded for use as a skating rink. The park is
serviced and maintained with the help of a lot of dedicated
volunteers. On the right side of Webb Street is the Lions
Club barn where they store equipment to be used in various
programs, including an auction. These places used to be a deep
pond, and for a couple of decades a dump. In the time before

Webb Street ran all the way through to State Street, there was an inlet here. I'm not sure of the timing, but at one point the rail viaduct went across this neck of water. Then it was sealed off, and the viaduct replaced by a rail embankment, and Webb Street extended through to State. Between then and the mid 1950's, what is now Lions Field was literally a dump. When I was a boy, my friend Bryce and I used to sell scrap metal to the man who ran it. Trash, garbage, and sometimes tires were burned here. To look at it today you would never know.

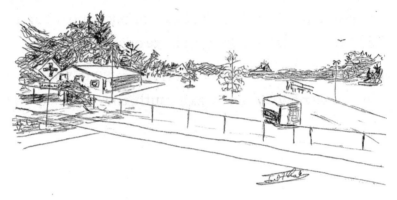

Lions Field Park

On the Lions 'barn side there was a deep pond between Webb and Merrick Streets. We were sure as kids that it was still connected to the river underground, because the level, which was about the same as the river, and

If you continue on Web Street to State, Webb becomes Graves Street south of the traffic light at State. This was added only at the end of the last century. For quite a while it was a blinker: yellow east and west, red north and south. When I lived on Graves there was no stop light - the only light in town was at Gay Head corners, where the lighted "Clayton" sign is. At the top of the hill is a large home on the left. I lived there with my brothers and parents from age 12 to age 18, when I went away to college at Syracuse University. You can now do something you might have damaged your car doing in the 50's - continue on Graves to East Line Road. I can't recall the exact time it was paved, but it used to be a narrow, rutted track with sharp stones and mud puddles in the ruts. After you pass the fire station on your left and the school grounds on your right you will see a large park. There is an entrance on the right, just before East Line Road.That is the Gordon Cerow Recreational Park. There is an Olympic sized outdoor pool and an arena in the distance, past ball fields and a large open pavilion.

tureland back then. The trees on it now are 80 to 90 years old, and quite large now. When I was a youth, they were saplings.

East side, Gordon Cerow Recreational Park ball fields and picnic pavilion

Turn right onto East Line Road to the main parking lot entrance on the right. There is another pavilion, and park grounds, with a large parking area for events at the arena and pool, and another exit to James street to the West. In front of you in the distance, the school I attended for twelve years is visible through the trees. It is now Guardino Elementary School. Back then it was Clayton Central School, K through 12. All the beautiful park land was pas never seemed to change. Today it has been filled, and you would not know it was once there.

Arena and hockey ink at Cerow Recreational Park.

Ink sketch from author's photo.Samuel Guardino
Elementary school, and a tree scape

St. Mary's on the West Edge of the park. Ink sketch from author's photo

Leave the parking lot and turn left on East Line Road, and again
left on Graves Street. Continue on Webb Street to Mary Street
and turn left. If you drive straight to the end, in two blocks you

will see the Town and Village offices on your left, and these views of the Central Park in town.

This park has large old shade trees in it. I couldn't say how old, as many trees in Clayton (a heavily forested town, actually) were killed off by the Dutch Elm Beetle in the 1950's and 1960's, then replaced with new ones. I cannot say which trees are replacements, but the most of these trees are quite large. As a boy I remember some of the trees on the North end of the park were crabapples, but I don't know if any of those are left. The park is quite shady in spots, with an open central area. In the first sketch you see outlines of a playground in the right center, under a large old tree. The upright and horizontal lines are the tennis court fence supports, and in the center to the Southwest is St. Mary's Church steeple, which.
is visible for miles, particularly if you are out on the river. Right below that sketch is another from a viewpoint just a little to the right (North) of this one. The reference photos were taken within days of each other.

The difference is the grouping of display tents around the center of the park, all the way to the edge in the front. The tents are for a weekly Farmers Market, held in the spring, summer and fall, where you will find paintings by local artists, arts and crafts. and fruits and vegetables grown locally, as well as souvenirs, jewelry and trinkets.

The Summer Farmers Market in the park

Drive around the one way park road from the Eastern side of Central Park halfway and come out next to St. Mary's on Mary Street at James. Cross James and drive all the way to the end, and park in front of or near the Antique Boat Museum, which is the subject of a later chapter. If you walk past the museum grounds you will be able to walk out on a heavy wooden dock extending into French Creek Bay. I should say "will be able to," as the 50 year old dock is being completely rebuilt, and will be finished in 2023. As a child, I would have been walking into the water at a boat launch if I did that. There was a private home just to the left, roughly where the Island Mariner Lodge is now. The Thousand Islands Yacht Sales and French Bay Marina now occupy land where a large wooden structure once stood. It housed a lively "Casino," in which show acts from all over the country used to play, and there was dancing. The dance floor remained, even under the bowling alley that came in after, and the many later years of boat storage on top of it once the bowling alleys were removed.

As you can see in the sketch, the Mary Street dock is fully equipped with streetlights and power and water stations for large vessels and small. Walk out there, and you will see one of the best views of Calumet Island there is. The houses on Bartlett Point almost look like you could reach out and touch them, and you will see the many fine yachts berthed next door to the Southwest at the marina docks, as well as the West side of the Antique Boat Museum. Mary Street Dock isn't really a park at all, but it will seem like one, as it is separated from the Boat Museum grounds only by a tall wrought iron fence, and by nothing on the waterfront. If you like crowds, and boats, and a good time, come here when there is something going on. It comes alive.

Mary Street Dock. Ink sketch from author's photo.

The next and last "park" is the Thousand Islands Land Trust's nature preserve at Zenda Farms. Zenda Farm's history is well documented, and I won't go deeply into it here. But when I lived in Clayton, and for many years afterward, it was an operating cattle farm, with two locations – this one and one on Route 12 toward Watertown, just south of Depauville. This one is just west of town on Route 12E, off the Bartlett Point Road. The sketch for this one is courtesy of my Sister-in-Law, Charlene Greene. We had enjoyed catching up on her patio overlooking the river, from her home on the west shore of Bartlett Point. She suggested I might want to paint the scene from an unusual spot. She drove me there in her golf cart. Carol elected to stay in the car, as the ride, Charlene said, might be a little rocky. It was. We drove out through a swath of freshly mown hay to a vantage point that proved to be quite different from the usual shot of Zenda. The sketch is below. It was a clear blue sky day, with big puffy clouds off over Canada. Typical beautiful day in paradise. I got to take a few shots. My earliest memories of that area are of being dared to jump out of the haymow to the concrete floor of the largest barn, visible to the right in the sketch. Not a treat for a skinny twelve year old with major dust allergies.

Zenda Farms. Freehand ink sketch over pencil

But to get to see it this way was a real thrill, and the

sketch was fun. I may watercolor it. For a place that doesn't have a lot of public spaces to sit, or parks, Clayton sure has a lot of parks.

DINING AND DRINKING

People enjoy eating out, having a cup of their favorite beverage, and just socializing, even if they live in a tourist friendly town year-round. But to qualify as a true tourist friendly place, there have to be places where people who are just visiting can congregate or just stop in for a bite. And there have to be enough, and of the right size, to accommodate people comfortably and quickly.

When I was growing up in Clayton there were lots of those places, some large enough to handle the crowds that got out of buses from New York or other cities where tour companies used Clayton as a destination, or a waypoint. Some were enough cater to the large numbers who disembarked from tour boats with an appetite generated by fresh river breezes and a long absence from land.

I worked in one of those places from 1956 to 1960, starting as a dishwasher and ending as unemployed, off to college. McCormick's was a Clayton institution, like O'Brien's, The Golden Anchor the Thousand Islands Inn and the Hubbard House. A boat could come into the dock right behind McCormick's and disgorge 50 to 100 hungry people, who came in for the Smorgasbord said to be famous worldwide. After partaking of the Smorgasbord, they could order fresh caught fish, aged steak, and many other specialties that Mr. Vincent Dee, the owner and a fine man, had advertised far and wide. While dining, most had the privilege of an excellent river view. But Mac's was not just a tourist trap with a vista, good bar and food. In the offseason parties, weddings, group meetings and local family dinners were a mainstay. On the right side of the photo next to the boat line you can see the former Waldron's Jewelry store building, which now houses Bella's. From a photo in the Thousand Islands Museum Archives. (Below)

McCormick's from the water, ca. 1950. Notice the tour boat at the dock.
Sketch from a photo from Thousand Islands Life Magazine

(Above) McCormick's from across Riverside Drive.

Bella's, ca 2015. iPhone sketch from author's photo

The boat line pavilion was just to the photo left of the sketch of Bella's. To the right was the Ellis Block. The empty lot behind the iron fence is now" Forever Park."Bella's has grown from a coffee and pastry shop with lunches to a full-service restaurant with the addition of a patio in the space where the boat line pavilion used to be. Originally there was an open wood deck at the back, with a killer view of the river. It is now covered and enclosed with clear plastic zip open panes for inclement weather. In addition to the covered patio a few steps down from the main level, down another stair, is an open patio practically riverside. On a nice day, the lower patio seats are the best in the house, literally outdoors, under a large tree. You can see a younger version of that old tree peeking over the boat line roof in the land side view sketch of McCormick's and the boat line pavilion.

When Carol and I first moved to Clayton for the summer of 2004 Bella's had not yet opened, and the building contained the Clayton branch of Uncle Sam Boat Tours and a gift shop. Carol worked there that summer and I worked in Alex Bay at a gift and coffee shop. Try not to think of me as a barista. I was not very good at it.

Inside Bella's, ca 2007. The windows in the background
look out at the river. There is a deck outside which was not
covered then. Digital Painting is from author's photo

The following summer Bella's had just replaced the gift shop,
and it was already very popular. I used to go there mornings for
coffee and a Napoleon when Carol went to work at the Magical
Swan in Alex Bay. I was unemployed for three weeks until I
went to work for Peter Mellon at Antique Boat America. I used
to sit on the back deck and have my breakfast, reading and
watching the river traffic. When I started work I had Sunday
and Monday off, and continued the practice, sometimes with
Carol.

Since that time we have been annual visitors, but rarely for
coffee. By 2012 I had started painting, and I began frequenting
my favorite sidewalk studio in front of another eatery.

In 2010 we started having coffee-and at The Scoop, right
across from Rotary Park. It's a great place to sit and watch both

river traffic and people traffic. Sooner or later everyone seems to walk by, and the coffee and deserts are abundant and good. Another plus is the position of the building relative to the summer movement of the Earth around the sun. It is always shady mornings on the sidewalk in front of the Scoop.

Since my medical regime says I *must* stay out of the sun, it is a perfect place to plant my easel and my derriere for a couple of hours of work and people watching. Most mornings someone I went to school with or have met over the many years we have been summer visitors will walk by. In fact, it is the only time I get to see most of them. We have found that most people have busy lives too!

The owner, Mary Zavistoski, is kind enough to let me sit out front and take up space while I do art. Sometimes people come by and comment, but mostly it's friends and acquaintances stopping to chat briefly, maybe over a cup of coffee and a pastry.

My favorite outdoor studio

It's a welcoming place, popular as a place to eat, have coffee-and, or, particularly in the evening, an ice cream cone. A good number of regulars come in by boat just for the latter. That's convenient because it is right across the street from the docks. Just a door down the street is a restaurant and tavern, The River Bottom Bar and Grill. I can't review it because we have yet to eat there. Our last visits to Clayton we rarely ate out, as the Pandemic has changed our perspective on doing so. Next door to that is The Little Bookstore, where you could buy my last book, PK, Growing Up Tame, if so inclined.

Digital drawing of Carol and me, having coffee-and the morning
before leaving to return to Cumming, GA

Across the street where the spa used to be is a popcorn store, which just moved across the street from next door to The Little Book Store. Next door to the popcorn purveyor is another restaurant, Attilio's. The back door of Attilio's leads out onto a covered wood deck, as I have mentioned before, (See sketch of Rotary Park Waterfront) where you can consume your pizza and beer with a great view of all that goes on at the floating docks below and out on the river. It's a good place to sit and watch the sunset too, if you time it right.

Just down the road on the south side, after you pass the Opera House and the closed Thousand Islands Inn, is a parking area for the health club on the corner. If you walk South through the lot you will see the entrance to O'Brien's Restaurant, just as it looks in the sketch below. O'Brien's is a large venue suitable for parties or meetings or just casual dining. There is a bar where they sometimes have music, but always seem to have fun. It's open year-round, so it's a favorite with the locals. In 2010 we had our 50th CCS reunion there, and Carol and I have had dinner there occasionally. If you're lucky you can score a parking space in the lot fronting Riverside Drive, but on weekends it is always popular, and crowded.

O'brien's Restaurant

Continue on down the same side of the street and you will see the front entrance to the Thousand Islands Harbor Hotel across Webb Street. The hotel has a beautiful bar, patio and restaurant overlooking the river. Tables are limited, as is outside seating, so it's best to have a reservation. This is a great place for dinner in the evening, as it's not usually noisy, and the river is right there in front of you. At night you can see the lights on the Thousand Islands Bridge downriver. After dining you can take a stroll on the river walk. Turn left for Frink Park, right for the marina docks. If you come by boat and your vessel is equipped for overnight stays, you can book a space on the piers, complete with water and electric.

Reversing course back down Riverside Drive you can dine or have desert at Di Prinzio's, which as mentioned before, has a nice, nearly water level patio as well as indoor seating. Again, like the other dining venues, it's best to have a reservation. We have not been able to dine there yet, but I hear it is excellent.

DiPrinzios store and restaurant. Ink sketch from author's photo.

If you continue down Riverside to John Street and cross to the south side you will see an impressive Victorian home which has been converted to a fine dining establishment. The Johnston House was originally built by a Captain Johnston, a river and lake freighter captain and later ship builder in Clayton at the end of the 19th century, beginning of the 20th.

The house has survived at least two major conflagrations, one of which left it the only building standing at that end of Riverside Drive. It has been converted to a restaurant and party facility and is also occasionally a music venue. Dining is indoors and outside in the garden. Carol and I have not eaten there as yet, but I hear good reviews.

The Johnston House

A walk back across Riverside Drive will take you past Channelside Restaurant. We eat here every summer at least once, because the food is good and the view from the back deck is superb. It's now covered, so you'll be in the shade, and as at Di Prinzio's and Bella's, you are looking right at the ship channel and Calumet Island. Like most of the other restaurants in town, the building is one I remember from my childhood, with a different occupancy. You can't get a reservation here, and there is often a line to get in, so arrive early and get put on their list. It's worth it.

We particularly like to go here with family for lunch. We have been lucky to hit nice weather the times we met my brother Jack and sister-in-law Marylou there, and it brings back river memories for both of us. The only thing missing is Calumet Castle, which of course isn't there anymore. But it's a great place to eat, and if your timing is right, you can sit and talk for a while, and watch the river traffic.

Channelside Restaurant. Ink sketch from a photo by Will Curtis

I think I may have mentioned that we like to do that already, but we do it whenever we can. Be sure not to sit too long, as people may be waiting for your table, or the servers may be wanting to clean up after lunch and take a break.Right down the street is the downtown location of the Coyote Moon.The main portion of the first floor is taken up by the tasting room bar, but you can eat here too. We like the view, from the deck out back, and the lunches. Be sure to try the wine, either here, or at their location out on East Line Road. Contrary to

Google's information on Coyote Moon, you can't get lunch out there, but the pleasant folk there are happy to serve you a wine sample or two.

Coyote Moon "Downtown"

Last summer we took our usual drive out East Line and decided that we would stop there for lunch. The young ladies behind the bar good naturedly informed us that no, the all-powerful search engine got it wrong. They only do lunch on special occasions, but we were welcome to go "downtown" and dine and taste at the riverside location. We did, but not before I took several photos to use as exemplars for a sketch of the front of the tasting room. Once again, the lunch was delicious.

Coyote Moon Winery and tasting room on East Line Road

Walk or drive back up Riverside and turn left onto James Street, the other Main Street in Clayton. On your right you will pass what looks like a gas station/convenience store. That's because it once was both in a past life. Now it is Mar's Pizzeria. It's one of the non-franchised (you won't find any franchises at all in Clayton or Alexandria Bay) places you can get pizza in town, and it's right on a corner with lots of parking for a quick pick up.

Next door, and I mean right next door, is one of the most popular places in Clayton, the Koffee Kove. "Meet me at the Kove" has been a catch phrase for locals, summer people and tourists alike for decades. Serving breakfast and lunch, the cove is a place where you can get traditional diner food, or just coffee-and, served cheerfully in a bead-board walled, nautically themed cozy atmosphere with lots of tables and windows to let in the sun. Since the street improvement/ overhead power line and pole removal, the Kove has installed tables and high stools for additional outside seating in good weather. You can even buy a mug that says you stole it there.

The Kove has a history too. It was once Cantwell's creamery, a small grocery and milk delivery business run by the Late Frank Cantwell.

Head down James Street to the intersection of Hugunin Street. On your right you will see a small two story building directly at the Tee made by Hugunin and James. This building used to be the Lyric Theater, later, in my youth, the Bertrand Theater. After it closed in the 70's it became a liquor store. Kathy Danielson bought it in the early part of the 21st Century and created a new space, calling it the Lyric Café. You can have coffee, teas, Lattes, gourmet pastries, lunch, and dinner.

New Kove exterior, with outside fair weather dining furniture

Interior of the Koffee Kove (digital sketch)

There is gallery space on one wall for local artists. Kathy let me show a few of my own paintings there one year. No one bought any, but it was fun sitting in the front window, talking to people.

Kathy makes the space available for meetings of artistically inclined folk, and meetings of small local groups in general, and of course, the flocks of tourists and Island People who show up every summer. As previously mentioned, I tend to take advantage of the shade in front of another local eatery when I paint in the morning, but the Lyric is also a good place for that. When my paintings were on display there, I spent an afternoon in the front window, working on a painting, available to talk with anyone interested. Lots of people looked at my work but did not find it worthy of purchase. Too expensive, probably, for an unknown artist. Story of my art career: everyone wants to have it, but only if I give it away. As an aside here I should mention that selling it is not all that important to me. I do it for relaxation, and fun. Be sure to stop in at the Lyric. You'll see theater memorabilia and art, and you can even sit upstairs on the balcony that was once the projection and film storage room. As a bonus, of course, the food and coffee are good too!

Looking East on Hugunin Street from the Lyric front window. Freehand sketch on iPad.

As teenagers, my friend Bryce and I walked from Graves Street to the movies in an ice storm, when it was likely the power would go out from lines coming down. It didn't. We walked the same route on another night where the temperature went down below -30, having not listened to our parents about the dangers of freezing to death. Did you know that if you spit at -30 the spit will freeze before it hits the ground? Probably you didn't need to know that. I saw my very first movie, the serial Don Winslow of the Coast Guard, then my first John Wayne movie and my first horror movie at the Bertrand Theater.

Inside the Lyric. The stairs lead to the balcony.

The above is an ink sketch for base of a watercolor painting of The Lyric Café the author did for Kathy Danielson. The utility pole the street beautification project insisted on leaving in front has been left out. One of the things an artist can do that a camera can't.

Continuing up James Street to Mary Street and turning right you will head back toward a part of the river known as French Creek Bay, or in more recent times, just French Bay. One block down there is parking on both sides of the street for the Antique Boat Museum. More about that later. Across the street, at the corner of Alexandria Street

The front deck of the Wood Boat Brewery

and Mary, stands a large Victorian house converted to a brewery and restaurant. The Wood Boat Brewery makes some fine beers and ales, I'm told. I say "I'm told" because I am not able to drink any beer, wine or spirits with the medication I take every day. Thus I rely on Carol's taste in beverages. They also make some good food there, and you can enjoy it inside in the bar, or outsIde on the massive deck that surrounds the front of the building.

There is a private dining room upstairs as well for parties and meetings. The deck is roofed across the front, with open areas to the sides. It offers a view of the Sea Way channel across the waters of the inlet where ships used to be constructed, and the docks of the Antique Boat Museum on the other side of the street. Where the museum parking lot is now was a vacant lot next to a knitting mill when I was a youth, and there was a beach on the water's edge. The polio epidemic in the 50's put an end to beach activity there, at least as far as my family was concerned. We used to rent the cottage three doors up Alexandria from the brewery, and last year we rented Kathy Danielson's cottage two doors up from that.

Below is the view from the Deck of the Wood Boat Brewery. The Boat House is center-ground to the right, and you can see we had a great view of the museum and the river from there as well.

Nearly every year we have our first meal out at the Wood Boat Brewery, sitting about where the next sketch viewpoint is, looking at the river and the Antique Boat Museum. We also rented an apartment owned by the Muggleton family, over a boathouse on Riverside Drive, just out of visibility to the right in the same sketch. The brewery is an easy walk from there too.

There is a restaurant that just reopened under new management that I should mention here. Due to the two year pandemic hiatus in our Clayton visits we have not been able to eat there yet. I don't have a photo to sketch from, except the old one that is available on Google Street View. It's called the Island Bay Pier House, located on the North side of State Street at Mercier Avenue. We pass on the way in and out of town on State Street, or down Mercier Ave. to take our annual drive around Steele's point. My father kept his boat in a private boathouse on Steele's Point for a couple of years, and I (I'd say we, except I'm not sure how Carol feels about it) have always enjoyed taking a spin out to the end of the point and back to see what has or hasn't changed. Maybe this Summer we will get to dine there.

Island Bay Pier House

The restaurant in the above sketch is located right across State Street from the Clayton Golf Club, where my friend Bryce and I used to collect and sell "ponded" and "roughed" golf balls as a boy. The club managers, Mr. and Mrs. Bertrand, were fairly tolerant of us. That is if we didn't get in the way of the people playing the course. We and the other kids were a good source of used golf balls. I also used to play golf, rather badly, on the course when I got older. Right across the State Highway is The Clipper. You could hit a golf ball into the parking lot, but of course the tee is not pointed that way.

You can check out the Clipper menu on line, as you can with other dining establishments already mentioned. In the decades we have been in Clayton. For the summer or just a few weeks, we have never had a bad meal there. In fact, we have enjoyed quite a few good ones.

Natalii's Restaurant, sketched from a photo on their website

On Route 12 south, coming into or going out of Clayton, you will find Natali's C-Way Restaurant. This place has been a traditional watering hole, gathering place and family restaurant for generations. It has grown over the years and now includes a golf course and a motel. Carol and I have eaten there for years, and my high school class has held three reunions there. There is a large room on one side suitable for meetings and gatherings like weddings or reunions, and a large room on the golf course side for restaurant seating. The bar facing Route 12 also has seating with view windows. I highly recommend the traditional Perch dinners on Fridays in season. Best known is the Italian food. There is a weekly Pasta on the Green charity event. It can be crowded for dinner so again, reservations, or get there early.

Last, but not least is the Chateau, a restaurant opened in the last decade in what used to be a nunnery, then a private home, and I believe a B&B. In its current form it is a high quality restaurant catering to fine dining and parties. It is also on the grounds and shares ownership with Clayton Spirits, a distiller of "Straight Bourbon Whiskey." I used to fantasize a lot as a kid when we drove around the area with our parents, and later, when I drove around the area without my parents. It was somewhere between fantasy and a daydream. I always wanted to see what it looked like from the water side, close up, and to live there. Until the restaurant opened I could only see it from Route 12E as we passed, or from the water if we ever got that close. A couple of years ago before the pandemic our friends from Canada, Bernie and Margie, joined us for lunch there, and we plan to again. We ate out on the open patio – on the riverside. Dream come true! Not only was the view as spectacular as we thought it would be, the food was very good. It was just lunch, but yum. We did not get the chance to go back last year, as we were trying hard to fit every thing we missed the year before into two weeks, after we drove all the way from Albuquerque to Clayton, and faced a 5 day trip back. We missed our Canadian friends as well. They will be back this year.

We didn't get the chance to tour the distillery, but we did visit the tiny chapel on the property. It is a beautiful spot, and I would love to attend a mass there one day.

The Chateau and Clayton Spirits on the Cape Vincent Road, State Rte 12E

I hope you have enjoyed this chapter on dining out, just snacking or desert. In a later chapter I will get into stores and restaurants that are not around anymore, and stores and attractions you really need to see if you have the time. I won't make a recommendation for any of the eateries I've mentioned here because I don't know each reader's taste or finances, nor the time you will have available on your visit. But I urge you to try them all, if you have the time. You won't be disappointed, I think. Even if the food doesn't suit, the killer views more than make up for that possibility. I think you will like them all. We do.

CASTLES AND ISLAND HOMES

I have told you all I personally know about one particular Castle, Calumet, and its influence on me and on Clayton. Castles have always been important to me. I saw and heard about two great examples almost every day as a boy. In 4th grade and beyond I drew castles every spare moment, it seemed. Later in life I visited quite a few. Carol and I visited Windsor Castle, Arundel Castle and Clifford's tower in England, and Harlech in Wales in 1992. My brother Jack and I visited six or seven more in Wales in 1993, including one that was Welsh built. Carol and I also visited six castles and 2 Chateaux in France and Hurst Castle in California. Fortunately I have a very patient wife.

My brother Jim took me to visit Calumet when I was around 10, and we roamed around inside like tourists. By then, in 1952, the ballroom had extensive water damage. I recently learned that the ballroom was disassembled and moved to a church building in Watertown. We went to see it once, but it was closed to the public at the time. I still want to see it again.

In about the same period my brothers took my dad's Lyman and went to Boldt Castle, taking me with them. All I recall about that trip was being terrified half the time as my brothers told spooky stories, none of them true, about the castle and why it was abandoned. It was severely vandalized, and pieces of the expensive construction, such as mantels, had been removed. They probably could be found in other places today. The castle remained in that heavily damaged, unfinished state until the 1960's. There were tours, but it was not like today. When the Castle was taken over by the Thousand Islands Bridge Authority, to be run as a tourist attraction, monies were allocated for preservation, restoration and new construction. These aligned with the extensive blueprints available after construction was halted when Mr. Boldt's wife passed away suddenly. Since he was building it as a monument and a tribute to her, and she was now gone, he told all the workers to drop their tools and leave. They did, never formally returning, until the T.I. Bridge Authority took it over. Work continues to "restore" the original. It actually goes far beyond restoration. It does and it will look like it was intended, per the plans.

I won't go into any more detail about the castle here as you can, and should, look up Boldt Castle on the internet, at the 1000 Islands Museum in Clayton, or on a tour of the castle itself. I highly recommend the latter. We do it nearly every other year, sometimes from the Boldt Boat House on Wellesley Island, sometimes from Alexandria Bay, both on Uncle Sam boat tours.

Above is "Bolt Castle," in a Grayscale rendition of the first painting I ever sold, in 2012. Acrylic on 16x20 canvas. The color version can be seen on my art page at Fine Art America where you can purchase prints and merchandise with this painting on it. (https://joel-charles.pixels.com//

I have included a few of my Boldt Castle paintings and drawings in this chapter. I could have done an entire chapter on Boldt but chose instead to whet your appetite for a tour in person. Don't miss it. Believe me, it is worth doing.

The original sketch on canvas of the castle, from author's photo. The original is under layers of acrylic paint, but prints are available.

Below is my painting of Ewloe Castle in Wales, from a photo I took while touring castles in Wales with my Brother Jack in 1993, accompanied by our very hospitable Welsh Cousin Beryl and her husband, Elwyn. It is included as an example of my fascination with castles. Ewloe is a ruin, havingbeen destroyed centuries ago in one of the many conflicts to sweep Wales at the time. It is the best preserved of any Welsh built castles in existence. Most of the existing castles in Britain were built by the Norman conquerors and their descendants.

(Above) iPad sketch of the castle and Alster tower from the channel, from author's photo. (Below) Ink sketch of Alster Tower at Boldt Castle from the land side from author's photo.

The photos of sketches and paintings included, Except for Ewloe, are of popular subjects on Heart Island, formerly Hart Island before Boldt named it for the romantic aspect involved. In the next sketch you see a statue of a Hart, a species of deer. There is also a Hart statue found on one of the Castles's gabels facing the lagoon and the water gate. People have been known to climb up to the hart and sit astride it for a selfie. I would not suggest doing that.

The power house above is below the water tower, and isolated on a separate man made Island, connected to Heart Island by an arched stone bridge. It's part of the tour. You can tour nearly the entire castle, the Power House, water tower and rookery, and parts of Alster Tower. The latter was built as a playhouse for Boldt's and guests 'children, and included a bowling alley. The great, inexorable St. Lawrence rises and falls to produce both low water and floods, and as with all river front property, Heart Island has had its share of hydraulic damage. It's location makes Alster Tower on of the most susceptible buildings on the island. Over the years extensive leaky roof damage, and below the waterline erosion and hydraulic damage to the very foundations of the building, has made the interior tourist unfriendly, if not downright dangerous to the survival of the building itself. Heroic efforts to reverse and reduce that damage have resulted in the increased ability of the building to withstand the elements, and increased accessibility. Unfortunately, crowds of people being what they are, steps have to be taken to prevent the visitors to the building from loving it to death. It's enough to say that if you can get in to see it, be sure to make the walk down from the castle to see what is being and has been done. The same goes for the Power House.

Boldt Yacht House, grayscale print of, 12X24 acrylic on canvas,
from a photo by Dale Hull, with permission

(Above) iPad digital painting of Boldt Power House, (Below) grayscale
print of "Water Gate," watercolor, both from author's photos.

Water Gate at Boldt Castle heart shaped Lagoon. Grayscale
of Watercolor from author's photo

BOLDT CASTLE

Ink sketch of Boldt Castle from the passenger terminal area

Ink sketch of Boldt Yacht House

Downriver there is a slightly newer castle also open to the public. Singerer Castle is located just over the Canada United States border on the U.S. Side. Built in 1905, it was continuously occupied until the mid 1960's. At a cost of about $500,000 in 1905 dollars, it too was built as a surprise gift for the wife of a wealthy tycoon, Frederick Bourne, the 5th president of Singer Sewing Machine Company. It is now fully staffed in the summer as a tourist attraction, wedding venue, and occasional movie set. One can arrange to spend the night in the castle for a price. Carol and I visited the castle from Chippewa Bay in 2010, and the painting I did of it from a photo taken as the boat returned to Shermerhorn Landing.

Singer Castle, Grayscale photo of acrylic on canvas
by author from photo by author.

The sketch the author did on canvas for the above painting

Be sure to check out the official Singer Castle web site for the castle on the internet for more information.

Back upriver from Boldt was Pullman Castle, Castle Rest. Like Calumet and Boldt and Singer castles, Pullman was built by a tycoon. George M. Pullman was famous and made rich by inventing and building Pullman rail cars of a type to transport the same folks who were even then visiting the Thousand Islands by Rail. I have never shot any photos of the modern day Castle rest, so have never sketched it, but if you Google it you will see Ian Coristine's photo. Today it more closely resembles the rest of the large Victorian homes built along Millionaire's Row just upriver from Alexandria Bay. Most of the original "castle" is gone. Infamous for the "Pullman Strike," Mr. Pullman was quite prominent in the 1000 Islands as well. Many famous people and dignitaries were known to frequent Castle Rest, including U. S. Grant and Clara Barton. The Pullman family owned four islands, including Hart which they sold to Boldt, who renamed it Heart Island. It is fairly reasonable to say their family was influential in getting the 1000 islands known as a destination.

View from the veranda, 16X20 acrylic on canvas by
author, from author's 2017 photo

Not far upriver is Cherry Island, once owned by the Pullman
family. One of the big Victorian homes, on the island now
a popular destination for cruises and parties, Casablanca
stands out on the foot of Cherry Island like a white swan,
surrounded by a vast semicircular verandah, with a view
down river toward Alexandria Bay. Clayton Island Tours visits
this elegant home, now Occupied by Philip Amsterdam, who
hosts occasional charity events and parties. Carol and I were
lucky enough in 2017 to

Casa Blanca

Sketch of Casablanca from author's photo taken in 2017

Gargoyles on the lawn at Casablanca. iPad sketch from author's photo.

book one of the tours It included a buffet seating on that very verandah, and a telling of how our host's family acquired the mansion, and other tales.

Cherry Island Mansion Twin Pines, ink sketch from author's 2017 photo

Author's sketch of Frontenac Hotel, from an old postcard

As you move back up river after your tour at Casablanca, you will see these old homes once again, and as you pass between Round Island and Little Round Island, you will see many slightly smaller versions, and more modern "cottages" built on Round Island, and in the last few years, on Little Round Island. You will also pass the which has served the Island continuously since the turn of the century. I believe you can still mail a letter there, postmarked Round Island. The post office is located at the spot where boats landed for the Frontenac Hotel, built and owned by Charles G. Emery, the same tobacco magnate who built and owned Calumet Castle.

(Above) Round Island Post office, (Below) Calumet water tower, iPad sketchs from author's photos

Calumet Water Tower, iPencil sketch from author's photo shot in 2017

Don't leave the 1000 Islands without a boat tour. I recommend the one from Clayton Island Tours, but a real treat is taking both theirs and Uncle Sam Boat Tour's in Alexandria Bay. Come and stay at the river for a week or two. You won't be disappointed.

Calumet Water Tower from upriver, near sunset.

iPencil sketch from author's photo shot in 2017

Quick ink sketch of lighted Calumet Water Tower at sunset,

with risen moon. I never tire of this sight.

Calumet Lagoon. The boat we came in is at the end of
the dock. iPad sketch from author's photo.

PLACES TO STAY

Clayton 1000 Islands Harbor Hotel, as seen from the dock at Frink Park.
I think the Architecture fits in with that of the island homes above.
Grayscale photo of 16X20 acrylic on canvas by author from author's photo.

One of my earliest memories of motels is the sight of two cabins turned over, blown off their foundation, by flat winds from Hurricane Hazel. Hazel passed far west of Clayton, but the wind came down the lake, and then down the river with enough strength to bring down power lines and rip off the occasional roof. And turn over the occasional building. I can't recall which establishment it was, but it was near Mil's Motel and Cottages and Lanz's Motel. I was 12 in 1954 and Hazel was the first memorable hurricane I ever witnessed. I wish it had been the last.

I say that because in 1972 our town at the time, Elmira, was hit by Hurricane (then Tropical Storm) Agnes. One never forgets their first major flood, and we were right in it. Our street had about 10 feet of water on it. Our apartment upstairs was not flooded, but we had to move. Our landlords the Senkiws were flooded out. I was in the insurance business at the time, and could not get away from its effect it for years.

Why mention storms in this chapter? Because it deals with places to stay, places that sometimes themselves get storm wracked. Hotels and motels, at least in my memory, have always been safe havens. Places to go for a relaxing time, or places to shelter from the storm. In this chapter I will be putting the former first, because when you go to a tourist Mecca, you need some place to base. You need a "return to" after a day on the water, a day looking for antiques, or a day finding the best places to eat.

Hotels in the early days were a commercial mainstay for Clayton and other surrounding tourist towns. And in the '50s, when cars and buses became the primary transport mode for tourists, a thing called a motel sprung up – sometimes around the full to capacity hotels and "tourist homes." The latter hardly exist anymore, and have been replaced in many cases by short term rentals and B&Bs.

The first I will mention of the short-term rental variety belongs to the Muggleton Family. I grew up with Chris Muggleton and Lue (Ingerson) Muggleton. We went to Clayton Central High in the '50s. Nearly every year we lived in Clayton or visited afterward; we have spent time with them. We've remained friends, despite long absences and distances. They have often welcomed us into their home when we visited. A couple of years, after we stopped living in Clayton in the summer and just visited for two weeks, Chris said he wanted to rent us the Boathouse next time we came. In August of 2011 we arrived with plans to take advantage of the 4-bedroom space with family and friends invited to fill the place with fun and laughter, meanwhile enjoying the beautiful view and convenience of near downtown.

We had a great time. But remember the hurricanes at the beginning of the chapter? Between the last week of August and the second week of September, not one but two hurricane tail ends passed through upstate NY, still as hurricanes. Irene, then a lesser storm the name of which

The Boathouse (left) – grayscale photo of author's
8X10 watercolor from author's photo.

I can't recall, passed through parts of New York State. All our guests said no, they were not traveling in the likelihood the storms being as bad as they feared. The weather was not that bad in Clayton, and except for a few days of rain it was little different than our normal vacations on the river. But where our friends were, it was awful. Mostly flood-generating rain, but for people in the southern tier of New York, the fear of "here it is again,"

The boat house, iPhone sketch, from author's photo

was enough. We enjoyed our solitude, bouncing around in a huge apartment, listening to the waves slosh down below in the boat slip, and the rattle of the wind vane in the porch ceiling circling like mad. Chris said it never worked right after that.We missed 2012 in Clayton, as we had just moved from Tucson to Alpharetta, GA, and decided not to go anywhere that summer. We had two weeks at the boat house again in 2013, and they were Idyllic.

Freehand ink sketch of the view of French Creek Bay and the
Gas dock from the Boathouse front windows.

But by then we realized that all of our friends had lives too, and they didn't include driving to Clayton to visit. Thus we ended up driving all over New York to visit them. We really did not need so much space that year either.

In 2014 we spent the week of our anniversary in New york City, staying in a 44th floor apartment in Jersey City for a week. We had a great view of the city across the river, including the new World Trade building. But it wasn't Clayton. We went on to Clayton and since the Boathouse apartment was not available, we relocated two blocks South to the "Burd House," which we rented from the Kings, who had just bought it from the Burds. We enjoyed it there for 5 years, until the Pandemic came along in the winter of 2019-20. I am immune compromised, and

Carol has Atrial fibrillation, so to avoid public travel, we spent two weeks that summer of 2020 at a nice cabin in the Blue Ridge Mountains, at Blue Ridge, GA. Only a half day drive away. Beautiful spot, but it wasn't Clayton.

We decided we would travel again in 2021 and found that the "Kingfisher Cottage" was no longer available. Our friend Kathy Danielson, owner of the Lyric Café, has a cute little two-bedroom cottage behind her home on Alexandria Street, just two doors up from the Kingfisher, so we stayed there. It was delightful. We had made reservations to fly, and that Friday we were due to leave from Albuquerque a hurricane/tropical storm system hit Texas. We seem to be hurricane inconvenience prone. We were not going to be able to get out of Albuquerque until the following Monday, as the entire system got backlogged. The airline told us they could not even guarantee Monday, so we went back home, had lunch, packed the car and drove East as far as we could before dark. Amarillo was our final stop for the day. It took us four full days to get to Clayton.

The Kingfisher B&B. The rental cottage we had for five years is in the back, behind the car in the driveway

We arrived on Monday afternoon, and let ourselves in, with our luggage and groceries. We were exhausted, but after a quick meal we went down to the river to spend a delightful few hours with friends. When we returned Kathy was there to greet us. We had a great stay. This time we decided that we would not go anywhere that required much driving. We had already done 2000+ miles in four days, and were tired of being in the car for days. Instead of traveling we spent most of the time in Clayton with friends and quality porch time "at home." The great thing about all the places we have stayed, for me anyway, is their placement relative to the sunshine.

The porch at Kathy's Little Cottage on Alexandria street.

Like my favorite outdoor studio spot in front of The Scoop, they have in common just the right amount of morning shade, and not too much sun from noon to around four. Kathy's place comes equipped with a big table umbrella, to extend the shade.

In the past 60 years, 57 of them with Carol, I have stayed at many places in Clayton. That would include State Parks, but mostly in motels, with roofs, indoor plumbing, real beds and TV. There are many of these, both in and around Clayton. I don't mean to slight the ones in which we did not stay, but since we have not stayed in them I would not be able to review them fairly.

The first I'll mention is the C-Way Inn, which you pass on the way into Clayton on Route 12. When I was a child, this was only a restaurant and later grew to "resort" status. There is a pool, and several different types of rooms, right across the road from Natali's Restaurant, and the C-Way Golf Course. Carol and I stayed there in 1970, when my 10th Clayton Central class reunion was at McCormick's.

Kathy's Little Cottage on Alexandria Street, Clayton.
ink sketch from author's photo

K's Riverview Motel and Cottages. Ink sketch from motel web site photo

I remember that reunion well for two reasons. First was that Mary Lue Muggleton had convinced me to "MC" the festivities, my first time doing that. Second was the phone call I got from my mother, Ruth Charles, who was babysitting our 2-year-old son Kevin back at the C-Way. He had locked himself into the bathroom. She contacted someone at the desk and got him out.

We were back at the C-Way for the 2000 reunion, this time a combined class of 1959,1960, 1961 gathering. Kevin was 32 by then, so would not have needed a sitter had he come with us. I recall playing golf with Hank Recor, and being too late to take Carol out to lunch, but right on time later for my third engagement as MC. We would have stayed there for our 2010 reunion, but we wanted to be in town that year. The preceding week we had rented a cottage on Cayuga Lake at Longview Cottage near Ovid, NY. We thought we'd try to recreate the times we had spending two weeks every summer for 14 years at a Seneca Lake cottage. It was nice, and my brother Jack and his wife Marylou came by for an afternoon.

Grayscale print of 9X12 Watercolor of the C-Way Inn and pool

But it wasn't the same, and it wasn't Clayton. I wanted to get back there, and since we were having our 2010 reunion at O'Brien's, it seemed fitting to stay at Bertrand's. Bertrand's is located in the middle of downtown Clayton. Right across from the Koffee Kove, not far from the Lyric, walking distance from the Scoop, and all of the in town restaurants mentioned earlier. Right down the street is Michael Ringer's Clayton Gallery, right next door to the Lost Navigator and just down the street from River Rat Cheese.

We booked a room for three nights right next to our friends Sara (DeStefano) Norton and Carolyn "Skeet" (Vincent) Bourgeois. Chris and Lue Muggleton picked us up and drove us the few short blocks to O'Brien's, and after the excellent reunion dinner the attendees all walked up the street to the dock at Rotary Park to board a Clayton Island Tours boat for a sunset cruise. When we returned slightly before the sun actually set, we joined our Bench O'knowledge friends (see previous sketch) to watch the actual event. And since the motel is not that far from the river, it was an easy walk back. The Bertrand as a great central location from which to enjoy one of America's best small towns. The day we left we got up early and walked around. I wanted to walk along the river, and Carol wanted to walk a ways toward Centennial Park at ground level on Riverside Drive. We agreed to meet at Memorial Park, and I set out down to the river bank, and a fog shrouded river. I had heard the mournful honk of a down-bound freighter while we were walking together, and I wanted to capture a photo of it.

Bertrand's Motel on a foggy summer morning by the river in 2010

I did, and if I could figure out how to sketch a nearly invisible ship in a field of foggy white, I'd include it here, but I'm still working on that, as you can see by the foggy morn at Bertrand's sketch above. The houses in the background are faint, but you wouldn't know it was foggy had it not been captioned.

If you hear a fog horn, try to get down to the river. Even if you don't see the ship, the sights are worth getting out of bed for. The fog usually burns off by 9 or 10, so it needs to be early.

When we stayed at the Kingfisher and Kathy's little cottage on Alexandria Street we often passed the Wood Boat Motel. We've never stayed there because we needed kitchen facilities and long-term accommodations most of our stays in Clayton.

The Wooden Boat Motel. Six cozy newly renovated rooms

But I remember it well for two reasons. It was there when I was a little kid, and it was right down the street from my friend Jim Marshall's parent's house. I spent a lot of time at Marshall's. Jim and Bryce Baker were musicians and had a band. They would quietly (without amplifiers) practice on the enclosed front porch, while I listened. It may sound corny, but I was their roadie. I had a driver's license, access to a car, and knew how to hook up the electronics when they played a gig. I was at nearly every one.

The other reason is I know the new owner. Pia Hogue lives in the house I spent most of my childhood in, before we moved to our own house on Graves Street. More about that later. She bought the Wood Boat Motel just recently, and has spent a lot of time renovating it, with themed rooms. From the photos it looks like she did a great job.

Just around the corner, down Union Street from Wooden Boat is Calumet Motel. This motel has been popular for years as well and has housekeeping facilities for extended stays. I have not stayed there and have no photos to draw from, but I understand that it is well managed, and has a long-time clientele among fishermen and tourists alike.

Back to 2002, when Carol and I first began our regular annual visits to Clayton. She was working for Alaska Airlines at Tucson International Airport as a gate agent. I used to watch her drive the jetway into position while being careful not to bang into the aircraft or knock of the vital Pitot tube next to the cabin door. The later was a firing offense. I felt like a proud driving instructor when I first saw her do that, but then I realized that a jetway really isn't like a car! She learned it on her own.

Because of her schedule with Alaska, and her lack of seniority, she could only get a week off that year. I left Tucson in late June, just before Monsoon season started, and she joined me a week later. We had reserved two weeks at Mil's Motel and Cottages, and I was hoping to convince Carol to consider buying a travel trailer and bringing it to Clayton every summer, where we could get jobs. The latter was possible because Alaska Air was closing its operations in Tucson, and Carol was not planning on moving with them. She liked Clayton, and visiting there, always has, but moving there was a different story. I was hoping that a week near the water would convince her that we could do it and enjoy it. There was to be a Clayton Central School all class reunion the following week at the Arena, and I had set myself a project for mornings while awaiting Carol's arrival. I used my phone camera to scan a stack of yearbooks my Sister-in-law Marylou had loaned me.

Mil's Cottages, up on the bald bedrock above the river

I set aside 2 hours every morning seated at the picnic table on the porch on the above sketch to scan what I considered to be the important parts of each yearbook from 1948 to 1960, the 12 years I was in school. I made a slide show, rented a large screen TV, (no flat screen and not very large) and played it at the reception desk at the reunion. Possibly two or three people looked at it. I still have the photo files preserved on two separate hard drives and look at them occasionally.

Mil's is a family owned and run place, with a fishing boat rental marina and waterfront cottages as well as the ones up on the hill like the ones above. I'd recommend it.

Our deck at Mil's Cottages. It was shady until mid-morning, and what a view. That's the American Narrows out front, lots of ship traffic, and sunsets.

Last year, 2022, we decided to change venue, and rented at K's Riverview Motel on Rte 12 toward Cape Vincent. We stayed in one of two cottage style apartments, this one in a 1 story bungalo just west of the motel itself. It is a two bedroom, two bath unit with full kitchen. There is another unit with a balcony that has a beautiful view of French Creek and the land south and west of Clayton. That one is on the second floor, and would have been impossible for us old folk to occupy. With that view I wish we could have! Our view was supplied by moving outside and sitting in a row of Adirondack chairs facing French Creek Bay and the marinas across the road, and those lining the shore along Theresa Street. I think I was out there for nearly an hour each day of the two weeks we were there. Our hosts Don and Linda made sure we had everything we needed. If you are just looking for overnight accomodation and don't need full housekeeping, the motel units are clean and well appointed, and you can't beat the convenient location if you are a boater.

I mentioned B&Bs, but I am really only familiar with one, and we have never stayed there, but would do so if we had to stay in Clayton for just a day or so before or after staying our usual two weeks in a short-term rental. Steven and Alyse Ritchie bought the old Blake house, formerly the McKinley House and did extensive research and renovation on the huge Victorian former mansion. They turned it into an exquisite B&B. You can find reviews on most travel sites, and it appears that people like to stay there. Steven and Alyse are gracious hosts, and go out of their way to make folks comfortable. We quite often see Alyse and sometimes Steven down by the river with our other Bench O'knowledge friends.

Alyse and Steven Ritchie's McKinley House B&B,
ink sketch from Author's photo

I wrote a piece about McKinley House and Steven and Alyse for the Thousand Islands Sun a few years back, and Alyse gave us a tour. It is one of the most convenient of Clayton locations, situated on the corner of Hugunin and John, just a block from nearly everything, across the street from the Post Office, and an easy four block walk from the Antique Boat Museum, the Opera House, all of the parks and most of the Churches in town.

I have saved the newest, and biggest for last. No judgements on the best, but this resort is in a class by itself. It is many things. It is relatively new, includes a restaurant and bar overlooking the river, many rooms (most with a river view), lots of parking, banquet and meeting facilities, and there is a Marina right in its front yard. It also employs quite a few Claytonians.

We have eaten there, but never stayed there. It is a little out of our retired people's budget. That said, it is comparatively, for what you get, very competitive. It must be, as it is often full, or nearly so. Have I mentioned the river view? One of the things we like to do is get a drink or dessert in the outdoor seating area. At dusk, after watching one of the St. Lawrence River's spectacular sunsets, you can see the lights of the 1000 Islands Bridge come on, along with thousands of gem-like boat house and home lights along the visible shores. You can see the same thing from Frink Park, for free, but you don't get the table and the dessert with it.

I have been fascinated with the resort's (official name 1000 Islands Harbor Hotel) development over the last ten years. We watched it grow in pictures, then in person one summer, and were pleased to visit in person the first year it was open. In 2014 the Muggletons treated us to dinner there for our 49th Wedding Anniversary. You never know who you are going to run into there. That night Chris and Lue had arranged a mini reunion with some of our CCS classmates. We were surprised. A couple of years ago we ran into a sports personality who shall remain nameless, and whom I did not recognize until we left. He invited us to sit with him and his wife, and we declined, as our group was otherwise occupied in conversation. I wish we had accepted.

My fascination has led me to draw and paint the resort many times. You see the resort stands in an area where I frequently played as a child while my dad fished off the coal dock. In later years the photos I took were of a vacant field, and the view therefrom. Then along came the resort. It is a strange, somewhat disorienting, but rather comfortable feeling to sit at a patio table and gaze out over the river through the eyes of an adult - past the big coal piles that now only exist in my memory. It's peaceful there, most summer nights, unless there is a wedding or other activity going on.

The River Walk, looking toward Frink Park, pre pavilion and before the resort was built. Note the Calumet water tower on the horizon. At the time, this was a parking lot. (IPencil)

This is one of the best places from which to view the sunset. You can also people watch, boat watch, and just relax in the environment here. There were some negative reactions to the resort. It blocks the river view for some; is only a seasonal employer; ("how in the world can they survive with the short season here?"), and one woman's comment to me on the street right after it was finished, Only my understanding of the wait staff's need to clear tables and seat other patrons keeps me from sitting there for hours. I was a restaurant staffer once, a bus boy. Watching them work keeps me from obnoxiously sitting there with empty glasses and an unpaid check, knowing they would really like me to leave if I'm not going to order anything else.

The current view from the patio at sunset, 2018. Lighted Calumet tower on the skyline. Digital sketch with iPencil on iPad

Recent resort freehand sketch, ink over pencil, from my photo in 2018

Recent resort free hand sketch, ink over pencil, from my 2018 photo

Gray scale print of 16X20 acrylic on Canvas, finished in 2018 from my 2018 photo

"What do you think of our new monstrosity?." Despite that, it has survived, and as resorts go, has thrived. Opinions wait to be confirmed. We like it.

I sincerely hope that you find a great place to stay and visit Clayton. It doesn't have to be any of the places I have covered. There are lots more in and around the village and town. These are only the ones with which I am most familiar.

BOATS

In the early part of the 20th Century there was no St. Lawrence Sea Way. There were few pleasure boats owned by ordinary folk. If you weren't wealthy and owned a boat, it was probably a fishing or work boat. Both could be used for fun and entertainment, but luxurious speedboats and cruisers were less common among ordinary folk. In the 1950's the big war was over, and boat manufactures who had converted to making military craft had to find a new market. Lyman Boat Works of Sandusky Ohio began producing a line of boats made mostly of plywood, which put them in the price range affordable by the not so rich but prosperous post war population. The lapstrake "clinker built" style of the Lyman dates back hundreds of years, but the material, marine plywood, dates to WWII when mahogany became scarce, and plywood with equal or greater strength and durability came along out of necessity. Today, of course, most small pleasure boats are built of fiberglass and plastic. To love wooden boats, one must also accept that boat maintenance is far more expensive with wood construction, even marine plywood.

I grew up watching boat pass on the river, both large and small. We were a family of four young boys when he and my mother moved to Clayton, and the river became an attraction. They developed a love for boats and the river. Dad used to take me fishing in rented boats from the marina at Glass Point. We would fish the marshy areas and small islands around Fishers Landing, a magical place on a bright summer's day.

Not content with being restricted to one area to fish in, Dad bought a 16 foot Lyman outboard, and later replaced it with an 18 'Lyman Islander inboard. I've written about both of these boats for the Thousand Islands Sun. The following is one such "story" the Sun published.

Grayscale print of author's "Fishers Landing Passage," 12X24 acrylic on canvas, from photo by James R Miller, with permission

My Love Affair with Boats

I have mentioned accompanying my boy, to the now Frink Park dock, when it was the dock left over from Clayton's past as a coaling station and ferry stop at a rail terminus. He also took me fishing at other land casting spots, one directly under the Thousand Islands Bridge at Collins Landing. Another story, perhaps.

This story is for all those who love boats. It is about how I came to love them, along with the river upon which I also love to see them float.

My dad did not acquire a boat until around the summer of 1952 or '53. Before that one of his friends sold him a 5 horse Evinrude outboard in 1948. He would put me, the motor, his little green metal tackle box, and two fishing rods with reels and hooks attached into the car and drive down to Grass Point. If there was an aluminum rowboat available to rent, he would carry the motor down to the water, lower it carefully onto the transom, and fill the tank on top of the motor with a little red gas can. Then we would go back to the car and get the rods and reels and the tackle box. After some fooling with the motor and mighty tugs on the cord that cranked it, away we'd go. Of course at a rate of speed commensurate with a 5 horse motor.

I was too little to fish, then, but I loved the boat ride. For one thing It got me off land where all of the things to which I was most allergic lived. But the other thing, aside from the pleasure of watching my dad expertly cast a line, was the blue water reflecting a sky filled with puffy clouds, and the reflection of green cattails on the water. Those days are etched in my memory, along with the smell of gasoline and oil, seaweed and wet rope, and the fishy smell of the minnows dying in the bait bucket we took along.

As I got older, I did learn to fish, though I have to admit the skills I developed did not carry me into becoming a lifelong fisherman. After I left the river in my late teens for my adult life I lost the taste for it somewhere, and never reacquired it. I still love to watch people fish, though. I guess it reminds me of growing up, watching my dad fish. But the boat thing, that never left.

Dad kept that motor in tip top shape, winterizing it every year and storing it dry, in the cellar clamped to a frame he built for it. We called it the motor box. In the spring he would take the 30-gallon drum he kept in the basement outside, fill it with water, and mount the Evinrude on the edge, in the water. He would de-winterize the motor, clean and re-gap the spark plug, and start it briefly. I watched him do this every year. I knew not to touch the motor. It was his pride and joy.

In the spring of 1951 or so, we were leaving to go on a shopping trip to Watertown in my parents' 1949 Ford. The day before, Dad and I had been out fishing, and the Evinrude was still in the trunk. He took the motor out of the trunk to allow room for groceries and things and set it on the driveway behind the car. At that moment my mother and grandmother came out of the house, and he went to help my grandma into the back seat. For some reason he reached back and closed the trunk after helping her and closing her door. I had gone around to the passenger side and opened the door, to cool it off inside. He told me to get in the car. I said, "But Daddy . . ." and he repeated, "Get in the car!", so I did. He started the car, and I said, "But Daddy," again. He told me to shut the door, so I did. He then proceeded to back up the car, accompanied by a grinding noise. He stopped and turned the car off, sat there for a few moments, realizing what the noise was.

He never blamed me or said, "Why didn't you tell me," or anything like that. Never. Of course, he was heartbroken about the motor. He took it and had it fixed, hammered out the dents in the cowling and lower unit, and soon, dented cowling and all, we were out on the river again. It never quite ran right after that though, and of course it didn't look as good.

In 1952 or '53 he bought a 16-foot Lyman runabout with a 35 horse Evinrude outboard from Harry Chalk in Fisher's Landing. That "Clinker Built" boat from Sandusky Ohio took us everywhere up and down the river. Gas was cheaper in those days. We spent a lot of time in the Lake of the Isles, and I loved every minute of the trip there and back in that little boat. My brothers got to drive it, and as they got older, took it out by themselves occasionally. Of course, their little brother didn't go along. I don't believe they were going fishing.

But when we all got to go out, or I went for the occasional evening ride with my mom and dad, I fell in love with the river without realizing it. I also fell in love with boats, and all about them. I read boating magazines and when on shore, sitting on the benches on Riverside Drive with my friends, talked about boats as we watched them come in and tie up. We talked about them as if we knew and understood their intricacies and idiosyncrasies, which some of us actually did. We could tell the difference between a Chris Craft and a Century and a Lyman and knew what lapstrake and V bottoms were all about. We had engine preferences and hull design preferences and the material used to construct all things marine. In some cases, we may actually have been right.

In 1956 or '57 my parents decided they wanted a bigger boat. They wanted to take a trip up and back on the Rideau Canal, and the 16-footer was just not big enough to be comfortable going so far, they thought. They bought an 18-foot Lyman Islander side steer with a 45 horse Gray Marine engine. My dad was an avid drift fisherman. It was how he caught his biggest fish on the river, aside from the huge great northern he caught off Frink Park. To do that it was best to start at a known point and let the river take you where it would. He was usually very careful, and quite good at it. He taught me how to do it, and how to pilot the boat so he and my mother could enjoy drifting along on a beautiful day, lines baited and waiting for a strike. We would drift, restart the engine, move upriver and drift again. Often, he would cast expertly, using one of his favored lures from the same battered old green tackle box he kept until the day he died, and the green steel rod on which he caught his biggest fish ever.

One day when they went out alone, they were fishing along the edge of Grindstone like that, and the engine wouldn't restart. By the time Dad got it started, they had drifted into shallow water, and the skeg hit a rock, followed by a bang. He immediately threw the shift lever into reverse and backed into deeper water, but the damage had been done. He dropped anchor out farther and shut down, diving into the cold river to look at the prop. It was damaged, but the skeg was intact and the shaft didn't appear bent. This was in the days long before cell phones, so all they could do was run slowly back to the marina and hope for the best. After a prop and bearing replacement and some bottom work, they were ready to go again, but I don't recall their drift fishing much after that, unless it was in a place where the water was deeper, or when I was with them to move the boat.

We had that boat until the summer of 1960, when I left for school at Syracuse. They sold it after that summer and moved to Syracuse as well. It was the last boat they owned, and I have never owned one bigger than a 12- or 14-foot canoe since. But I still love boats. I have rented boats, once a 22' fiberglass runabout with a 100-horse outboard in Florida, which I ran aground on a tidal sandbar. That is another story. Carol and I used to rent boats whenever I could convince her to do so, and once even rented a small houseboat in Canada; an experience about which we rarely speak. We have rented in Clayton, but the ride to Alex Bay through the Narrows convinced Carol that riding in a small boat under the Thousand Islands Bridge was not her idea of a good day. We tended to rent from Obrien's in the Bay after that. We still enjoy the trip into Lake of the Isles and around the Canadian side of Wellesley Island, but it must be in someone else's boat nowadays, as rentals have gone out of our price range as a vacation expense. We may rent a fishing boat from the Wellesley Island State Park Marina, if they still do that and there is a boat available. My brother Jack and I want to go to the part of the park that's only accessible by water, and just be two old guys fooling around on the water for an afternoon. It's been a while.

It's also been a while since I actually worked selling boats. While I didn't sell many, my three years at Antique Boat America are among my best "river memories."

Carol and I had moved back to Clayton for the summer in 2004 with our travel trailer. We both put our jobs on hold. I was an independent contractor driving for a bus company and a handyman/remodeling contracting company, Carol was a ticket agent for the Wildlife Museum in the Tucson Mountains. I did not work that summer at all, and had lots of time to roam free, taking photos of old memories. Carol worked at the gift shop for Uncle Sam Boat Lines in Clayton, in the space that is now Bella's.

The following winter I had five heart attacks, and a quadruple bypass. After surgery I called Jim Schnauber and his people built a beautiful deck next to our trailer at French Creek Marina, and after four months recovery from the surgery, Carol and I moved to from Tucson to Clayton in May to occupy it for the summer. I was perusing the Thousand Islands Sun classifieds daily the first week we were there, and on the day after I had dropped Carol at her new job in Alex Bay with the Magical Swan Gift Shop. I knew going back to work was a must.

I saw an ad in the classifieds for a salesman at Antique Boat America. Since I knew a reasonable amount about boats, and had 23 years 'experience in sales, I decided to apply. I went to their showroom and met Peter Mellon that day, and he hired me the next day. For three summers I worked with the crew there, taking Carol to work and returning to ABA, to open in the morning and leave in the afternoon in time to pick Carol up at work in The Bay. What I didn't know about boats already I learned from Peter and Doug and Warren over that first summer and got to put my physical conditioning back on track by moving boats around on the floor with an electric mule. Looks easy until you've tried it. I really enjoyed that place, and every year we go back there at least once, just to see the boats. I got to work two Antique Boat Shows in those years, and met a lot of interesting folks, both there and at the showroom on Route 12. I sometimes wish I could go back to work there, but rheumatoid arthritis has put an end to my doing heavy physical work, and our life in Georgia keeps us from moving back to Clayton in the summer.

Still, as I've written before, Carol and I will be found sitting somewhere along the River most days, perhaps in front of, the Scoop, our favorite riverside ice cream parlor in downtown Clayton. We both have a fondness for the river, and the people we leave there

when we go home. It's why she lets me keep the framed "Thousand Islands, A Portrait From Space" poster on our dining area wall, in every house we've lived in since, I'm sure. Also, we both share a fondness for boats, at least looking at them, anyway, although if I were to ask her nicely, I am sure she would go for a ride in one of the Antique Boat Museum's Hacker Craft reproductions. She feels secure in those. Probably something to do with who is captaining. We hope we see you in Clayton, this summer.

Headed in after a day fishing - Grayscale print, Lyman
8X10 acrylic on canvas from author's photo

That's the "little boat" story. Here are some other" little boat" sketches and paintings.

The Zipper is the most frequently spotted of antique boat tours. This boat is usually reserved for VIP tours, and it is so distinctive, both in sound and looks that it can be easily identified at a distance.

The Zipper, Ink sketch from Author's photo at
Antique Boat Museum boat show

The Pardon Me, a large Hacker Craft, also has a classic sound and look:

"Sometimes called "the world's largest runabout," *Pardon Me* is a fascinating study in yacht design. From a distance, she can appear to be an almost regular-sized triple cockpit runabout. Up close though, one can truly grasp her magnificent proportions. Though primarily a day boat for short pleasure trips, she also boasts a galley, enclosed head, and sleeping accommodations below decks. (Antique Boat Museum, Collections, Zipper

Pardon Me Ink sketch from Author's photo at
Antique Boat Museum boat show

"It takes some power to move this much boat through the water and *Pardon Me* was powered by a World War II-era 1500 HP supercharged Packard PT boat engine, which used nearly 100 gallons of high-octane fuel per hour."

(Antique Boat Museum, Collections, Pardon Me)

Hacker Craft have a long history about which much has already been written, and they have always been among my favorite boats, on the river or elsewhere. The company designs and name were moved to a new location in Queensbury, NY just north of Glens Falls near Lake George. New designs and custom work make the boats modern version of the early 20th century sedans and runabouts nearly impossible to tell from the real antiques.

Hacker Craft triple cockpit reproduction speed
boat and waiting passengers
at the Antique Boat Museum. Ink sketch from author's photo

Sleek new and antique models like this are seen on waters all over the country, and probably all over the world. I once got a call from a man in Utah who wanted to sell his Hacker. Antique Boat America could have brokered the sale and arranged for shipment of his boat to a buyer anywhere in the world. Since I was actually "retired" from Antique Boat America at the time, even though I was kept on the masthead of the ABA website, I couldn't help him much, so I put him on to the active sales people.

Sadly we did not have the time to take a ride on this or one of the other boats the museum has for rides this summer. Maybe next year.

Grayscale print, "My Dad's Lyman Islander", 11X14
acrylic on canvas, from author's photo

The above painting was re-imagined from author's photo of an identical 18 'Lyman taken at a boat show at the Antique Boat Museum. Her actual full name was Petit Argent Bouton (Little Silver Button) after my mom's dog. The transom is an artistic license version, removing the actual boat's name.

I have added a couple of extra photos of ink sketches from from past years of unnamed boats I found interesting. I can't find the citation for the first (it may have been Erin Green, but I believe it is one of mine) but I do have permission to sketch it. The second is from my photo of a "speedboat" docking at Rotary Park at around sunset, probably for a visit to the Scoop for ice cream. They didn't stay long.

Heading in - ink sketch at sunset from Frink Park, from author's photo

DOCKING AT CLAYTON
IN THICK FOG

ANTIQUE BOAT MUSEUM GAR WOOD
CRUISING PAST T.I. PARK

SAILBOATS

Author's brother Jim's Lightning. He sailed it on the River once, never again. Too many rude speedboat drivers, he claimed. Acrylic on 14X11 Canvas. RIP, Jim! We're sure you're sailing somewhere.

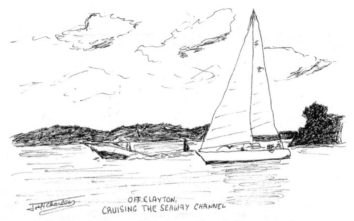

OFF CLAYTON,
CRUISING THE SEAWAY CHANNEL

Typical scene in front of Clayton. Sketch from my photo
taken from Chris Muggleton's boat in 2018

LYNX

Two masted schooner Lynx, a regular on the River.
Ink sketch from a magazine photo and memory of River background.

The Lynx motoring down-bound. Sketch from a
photo by Dan Blank, with permission

We see all kinds of sailboats, but the percentage of sailors is much smaller than power boats. Day Sailors are common, but you will never see a sane person sailing a sunfish or similar style boat out in deep water. Even kayakers and paddle boarders avoid doing that, normally staying as close to shore as possible. I won't go into Jet Skis, their owners seem to go anywhere they want. You really don't want to be in the Channel or in the St. Lawrence-Lake Ontario deepwater in a very small boat, as I found with brother Jim once, and never repeated the trip.

Boats like the Lynx are often seen on their way to or from a charter, used as school boats to train sailors, or on their way to Tall Ships events. Ships this size routinely sailed the St. Lawrence in the late 18th and early 19th centuries. There were small naval skirmishes in both the Revolution and the War of 1812, one of them in French Creek Bay.

(Above) Fair Jeanne, moored at the Antique Boat Museum. iPencil sketch rom autor's photo photo on returning with fishing with Bernie

Three masted schooner Picton Castle, a frequent visitor to the municipal dock at Clayton. Ink sketch from author's photo. There is a 12"x12 acrylic painting available for sale at https://joel-charles.pixels.com/

A magnificent sailing yacht, grounded at Thousand Islands Yacht Sales in Clayton. iPencil sketch from author's photo.

My sailing days are over, but I did get to sail quite often with my business partner and friend, Matt Perry, on both his Hobie Cat and his K-Boat on Seneca Lake, and with my brother Jim a couple of times on Cayuga Lake, the St. Lawerence and once on Lake Ontario. The later was a scary event on a kit plywood Sunfish Jim built. We sailed about 5 miles down the lake to a beach, had lunch, and discovered when we got back aboard the the drain plug in the bottom had come out while we were sitting on the beach. The boat had picked up about 30 gallons of water while we lunched, soaked up some sun and a couple of beers. We had to muscle the boat up the beach and let it drain. We couldn't drain it completely, but could sail back, albeit very sluggishly. By then the wind had changed and the necessary tacks took us a mile or so out into the lake, a bad idea on a sunfish. By the time we got back to the cottage, not having been able to see it most of the trip because of the 5 foot wave height, it was late afternoon. The wives were worried we had sunk or capsized. Never got on another sunfish.

I should mention that after one sail on Matt's K-Boat, Carol was put off sailing. She never took to the Hobie at all. Perhaps that was a result of the extreme angles involved in a heeling sailboat, or the fact that she watched a Hobie "pitch pole" in front of our cottage on Seneca Lake once. Our landlord and I went out in his boat and righted it for the crew by wrapping a line from one side of the boat to the other and down underwater to the mast, and using it to roll the boat upright. She was not impressed.

YACHTS AND LARGE
POWER BOATS

Yachts and larger power boats are also a treat to watch. The seamanship required to run one of these is much more complex than that required for a small craft like an 18-foot Lyman, but the basics are the same. When landing either one, you have to take into account the current, the wind, other boats, the depth of the water under your keel, and lots of other things that need your attention at a busy anchorage or dock. In 75 plus years of watching, I never tire of it. Anyone with the money can rent a boat, from a little aluminum fisherman all the way up to a 30-foot houseboat. They don't rent the expertise to go with the boat, however. Sometimes the outcome is funny, sometimes sad, but always entertaining. The most entertaining are the expert sailors, who come into the dock like they have been doing it all their lives. Some of them have been.

The next series of sketches and paintings is of larger power craft, even yachts, that can be seen docked or docking at Clayton, or often just motoring on by out in the seaway channel. The first one is an antique yacht at the Thousand Islands Yacht Sales storage lot in Clayton. It, like the sailing yacht in the last sketch, is grounded. I've always been fascinated by the way such boats are held in a vertical position on land. It always seems far too flimsy, but it is not. Simple physics is best. It takes up the least room and allows for bottom work while the boat is out of the water.

For removal or more ambitious repairs a sling or heavier cradle is required, but these spindly jacks are most often the norm. Large boat storage and repair operators have self-powered transport vehicles to get the boat out of the water and set it in one of these cradle arrangements. It's fun to watch if you get a chance. Yachts come in all sizes. Back in the 1920's through the 1950's large powerboats took the wealthy for cruises and carried guests back and forth to the estates on Islands up and down the river.

Then there were the large steamers that plied the St. Lawrence and the Great Lakes, carrying passengers from destination to destination, much like the giant ocean going cruise ships from the the last part of the twentieth century to the present. Some of them, like the Freedom below, are now configured as private yachts, and the

(above) Yacht of similar vintage to Kensington at Rotary
Park. iPencil sketch from author's photo

The Yacht Freedom moored at Frink Park, iPad
painting from author's photo

The yacht Freedom moored at Frink Park. iPad
painting from author's photo.

iPencil painting of Uncle Sam Boat Tours "Island
Duchess" from author's photo

old classic steamers are gone. Below is a Trumpy yacht moored next to the Duchesse houseboat at the museum.

Another type often seen in passing, and sometimes docked at Frink Park or Rotary Park, is the Tour Boat, like the Uncle Sam Boat Lines Island Duchess in the iPad/iPencil painting above as she appeared moored at Boldt Castle's tour boat reception dock, waiting for passengers to return. We took this boat on a tour once, but when you do Boldt Castle either from Alex Bay or the Boldt Yacht House on Wellesley Island you will take a much smaller done on an iPad, takes much longer than some of the simple sketches shown earlier. The wonderful thing about iPad sketches and paintings is that you can always erase or "paint 'over mistakes. That does not mean it is easy. Even the pen and ink sketches in this book don't classify as "easy," unless of course you weigh them against paintings like this. These are not converted photos or tracings of photos, but actual paintings, the only major difference is the medium.

SHIPS FROM ALL AROUND THE WORLD, AND SAFETY

Carol's favorites are the big ships that ply the seaway and the lakes. These range from ocean going cargo haulers to lakes freighters. The latter never go past the Gulf of St. Lawrence in Canada, but all of them can pass through locks and go all the way up to Lake Superior, the largest freshwater lake in the world, and the resting place of the storied Edmond Fitzgerald, a laker which went down in a gale in seas of a size you might see on the Atlantic. Of course, any of the Great Lakes have mean dispositions, at times. And they are all unpredictable, as is the St. Lawrence. If you plan to do any boating on the St. Lawrence, there are some facts and rules you need to know.

First, and foremost – although it is a great place for recreation, boating and fishing, this river can kill you. It's usually relatively cold, except in shallow places, or the surface of deep still water exposed to the sun. That means that if you have a boating accident, you might be in a place, or at a time, like night, where no one can get to you quickly. No one may even know you are in trouble. Hypothermia can set in. Or you may get ignored and drown from exhaustion. I've been out on the water and had an engine problem and people didn't realize we were in trouble. They may just wave hello because that's what they think you are doing. There is a reason boats have safety equipment, like air horn cans, floatation gear, lights, flares, etc. Even with that equipment, it is a bad situation if you're drifting in the Sea Way Channel – those big boats can't avoid running you down or at the very least, swamping you.

Get charts of where you are going. Places that rent boats may only give you a chart of the water around them. If you take one of their boats outside that area, you are going to be flying blind. The river is full of rocks. That's why they have these things all over the place:

Big ones like this are ship channel markers, but there are lots of smaller ones maintained by Save the River and other organizations. Some, placed by local cottage owners, may just be painted gallon Clorox jugs. The thing is, the water levels change from year to year, even from week to week, so the many (and I mean many) rocks and flat shoals that exist may or may not be a problem. If you have a chart, you can see that. Most people who own boats have a depth finder, and use it to monitor the water they are in. You shouldn't depend solely on that. It's still good to have a chart. That way you know it isn't a good idea to sail or motor along at speed through an area that is inches shallower than your keel or prop.

Don't go out into a storm unless you have a lot of experience doing that, and even then, you should run for shore as soon as possible. Waves are deceptive. A wave is measured from top to the bottom of the trough. Think of a sine wave that looks like an S lying on its side. In the sketch below the S has a bar dividing it in half horizontally to show that a 3-foot wave is only 1.5 'up, 1.5 'down. But the amplitude of a 6-foot wave is 3 up, 3 down That means if you are in the trough of a 6' wave, sitting in a 16-foot boat, you can't see over the top of the wave. You can't see landmarks unless you stand up. Waves on the St. Lawrence and Lakes are also tricky. They may be very close together, or there may be wide, large swells with waves on top of them, going in a different direction than the swell. On lakes like Ontario, and large, mostly shallow rivers like the St. Lawrence, waves tend to be closer together than the big rollers at sea. That makes them even more deceptive and dangerous if not handled correctly. People who have been around the river for years know these things and know what to do in these situations. If you just rented a boat, and your experience is mostly on small inland lakes, you could be in danger in a sudden storm or squall. They happen very quickly sometimes. Know your limitations. In doubt? Run in What looks like a good, calm water day can get ugly fast.

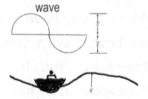

wave

Have a compass with you. Yes, you can get lost on the river if you don't know it well or have a chart. One low shoreline with trees against a skyline looks just like another shoreline. Without a chart to follow, and a compass, or known landmarks like St. Mary's steeple, or the viewing tower on Hill Island, you can suddenly find that you are not where you thought you were, and the bottom may not be where you thought it was either. I don't often bother with a compass, because I. have lived on this river, and know it well. Fog can however, suddenly make it impossible to see land, and the only way you can tell north from south is the direction of flow of the river. Don't go out without a compass when it might be like that. I have to confess I did that once, in a 14' rental. It was a terrifying mistake.

Do not get too close to the big boats. Even tour boats. They can not stop. A boat moving at speed develops something called "way." If a freighter is moving at around 12 knots in the channel (about 14 mph), even if the pilot throws it into emergency full astern, or just stops the forward drive of the engines, the ship does not stop for a long way. It's physics. "A body in motion tends to remain in motion . . ."

That's not the only problem with getting too close. You can't see it, but that ship is pushing a bow wave upwards of six or eight feet high. The slope of the wave is very shallow, so top to bottom it doesn't look like much. But it is a force, and there will be anywhere from 3 to 6 of them, one right after another, each progressively larger then smaller. The closer you are to the ship, the worse the swell, as they are closer together. I have a photo of a small power boat that is right up next to the prop wash and bow wave, practically under the stern counter of a ship. I have no idea why anyone would do that, and hope their outcome was better than it looked. A large pilot boat driven by someone who knows what they are doing can come alongside a ship easily if it's not too rough. You are not renting a large pilot boat. It is a lot easier to swamp a 16 or 18-foot runabout than you might think. Another thing – "following waves" of any great size coming over the transom can swamp an outboard boat, so you must keep moving if you are going the same way as the swell. Above all, if there are large waves, do not parallel them, as that could result in overturning your boat

183

if it's small enough. Where possible, quarter such waves. If the waves are that large, and you have little or no river boating experience, rethink going out today.

There are other things to think about, such as: be polite to fellow boaters; don't get too close to other boats at speed, especially fishermen and dive boats; know and obey the "rules of the road"; and *do not* drink while driving a boat. Always bear in mind that if you see a local doing something, they probably have done it for a reason, or out of necessity, or all their lives, and know how. You probably dont. If you use common sense, you'll be fine. If you don't, it can really ruin your day.

The variety of big boats out there is fascinating and informative. You can get an app for your phone to identify them as they pass up and downriver. Sometimes there is even information as to what their cargo is, and where they are from and where headed. Some are beautifully painted, some just gray or black work horses. They have been through locks, so you will see marks, like scrapes, on their sides above the waterline. The locks have bumpers that cause those marks, but they protect the ships, and the locks themselves. By law, the ships cannot be painted while in the water. They must stay in the water in order to work, so are not pulled regularly to be painted or refitted unless needed. In the course of a week or two you may see the same ship multiple times, or many times over a summer, and wonder why they don't paint it. That's why. If you like to sit on shore and get a great vicarious experience, check out the FaceBook page of "Ship to Shore Chef" Catherine Schmuck. She is a relief cook aboard the freighters that ply the Great Lakes and the St. Lawrence. She also writes cookbooks (Carol has one) and a children's book. Her photos and descriptions of the trips she takes are excellent depictions of life "at sea."

Age of Steam, ink sketch from photo taken in the 1950's, courtesy of Steve Shay. The photo was taken by his father.

Now for some ship pictures. The first is one was sketched from a photo taken back in the 50's by the father of Steve Shay, the Wood Shepherd. This is what most small coal fired steamers looked like back in the day, before diesel engines replaced steam. The white plume coming out of the stack is deceptive. It was black in the photo, and when I made a watercolor from the sketch, the plume was done in dark gray and coal black. No one really worried about coal smoke pollution back then.

Pacific Huron, passing under the Thousand Islands Bridge. That is ice on the rocks in the foreground. Grayscale print of iPencil painting from photo by James R. Miller with permission

The above digital painting was done from one of James R. Miller's photos that caught my eye on his site 1000 River Rats Now and Then, of which I am an avid follower because there are so many great photos, already composed well, that I can attempt to paint. This one captures the cold of an early winter day, when the SeaWay is still open , and the transit of a good sized freighter under the Thousand Islands Bridge, another of my favorite subjects.

I took the photo the next painting is based on from just downriver of the Rock Island light. The light would be to the left, with Wellesley Island behind the freighter, and the sun getting ready to set over the Canadian Mainland. Carol and I were on a Thousand Islands Tours group tour to Rock Island, which had just recently become a New York State Park. It is now one of the most visited parks in the area. "Team" is not the name of the ship, but the line that owns it. Unfortunately I was busy taking photos, and forgot to get the name of the ship in one.

"Team" Freighter down-bound past Rock Island Light.
Grayscale print of iPencil painting from author's 2017 photo

Bulk carrier down-bound under Thousand Islands bridge.
Freehand ink over pencil from photo by Jolene Tankowski with permission

The above photo is of The Viking Octantis cruise ship entering a lock. in the Welland Canal from Lake Ontario to Lake Erie. These have recently become more common again on the Seaway and Great Lakes. Ink over freehand pencil sketch from photo by Brad Wood, with permission.

Up-bound gas tanker passing Boldt Castle. Grayscale
print of iPencil painting from author's photo

WORKBOATS

Electric and Diesel car ferry Amherst Islander I up-bound
past Wolfe Island. Grayscale print of watercolor by author
from a photo by R.D White, with permission

The Amherst Islander is a new replacement car ferry for the Kingston area, Kingston to Amherst Island, in Lake Ontario. She is a "green" boat, both diesel and electric powered. Before the river crossing bridges were built, ferries were the only way to get across the river from Canada to the U.S. and back. And the only way to get to the larger islands in the river, or to the massive resort hotels. Now, as with Wolfe, Carleton, Howe and Amherst, it is still the only way.

Every winter, the tug below and other work boats bring in

the channel buoys like the one pictured earlier, and the same Frink Park dock in these sketches and photos is lined for the winter with the behemoths that mark the Sea Way Channel. They're there to help prevent accidents like the Eutarde and the Maplebranch, but sometimes the cause of the accident is not ignoring the markers – it is a result of mechanical failure, like a broken rudder or engine failure.

Buoy tug Robinson Bay at Frink Park Dock, freehand ink over pencil sketch, From photo by Dan Blank, with permission.

In any case, no loss of life that I know of has occurred here in a century. It was different in the 19th and early 20th Century, and there are wrecks to prove it. When there is a grounding or a ship anchors to facilitate repairs or offload cargo, tugs are on hand to help.

Clayton Fireboat "Last Chance" freehand ink over pencil sketch from photo by Tony Di Valentino, with permission. The boat was working a fire at a home on Murray Island when Tony took this photo.

As you might expect, the danger of fire on an island or a boat is always present. Accidents happen, and when you are surrounded by water, a land emergency vehicle can't get to an island, or a boat out on the water. People on the river with boats will, of course, help out where possible. But for bigger emergencies there are specialized boats, to fight fires or conduct water rescues. Fireboats are often seen in movies and TV spraying water in arcs over ships or boats to welcome them home, or in celebration. These boats have many more uses than that. Just within the last year, The apply named Last Chance was at a large housefire on Murray Island. They were unable to save the house, but with the Clayton and othere fire departments, and many volunteers, they were able to keep it from spreading to other homes. The Last Chance sketch above is from that fire, from a photo taken by Tony D.Valenino while she was replenishing water tanks. Firemen have a tough job. River firemen have it even tougher.

Workhorse of the Seaway, Channel Bouys -ink
sketch "Buoy 211" from author's photo

There are also barges with permanent cranes for dock and seawall building, and pile drivers, and dredges, pushed by small utility tugs, Then the ice comes. and there are ice boats – flat bottomed hulls with aircraft engines. At the beginning of the spring season ice breakers coem in to open the channel. There are boats of all shapes and sizes for many purposes. It's a busy river.

Work boat work horse – WWII Landing Craft conversion.
Quick ink over freehand pencil sketch from memory.

GROUNDED BOATS

In December of 1945, the up-bound Eutarde hit Chapman shoal. She managed to limp into the Consaul Hall Coal Dock at what is now Frink Park, but because of very heavy wind and waves was further battered into the concrete dock. The authorities feared she would sink at the dock, so she was moved farther out, where she promptly sank in about 20 feet of water (second sketch). She was later refloated, renamed and returned to service, but a later accident sank her for good.

In 1959 the gasoline tanker Maplebranch hit the same shoal, and did the same maneuver, but sank before hitting the dock. She rested on the bottom, only her superstructure showing, eerily like the picture of the Eutarde 14 years earlier. Paul carpenter and I drove down to see her misfortune after school that day. The photo has Paul standing on the dock with Maplebranch behind him, badly drawn, as usual. I really must learn figure drawing better.

The Eutarde, sinking at Consaul Hall coal dock, Clayton.
Freehand ink sketches from news photos

Paul Carpenter, (Author is not good at drawing people)
with the Maplebranch in the background.
Freehand ink over pencil sketch from author's 1959 photo.

.. ..

The Anna – a very special, much beloved boat

A few years ago I saw a photo of a grounded trawler on the
1000 Islands River Rats Now and Then FaceBook site. I asked
the photographer, James R. Miller, who is also the originator
of the site, if I could paint it. He agreed. I have drawn or
painted Anna a few times more since then. Anna is one of the
most photographed, painted, drawn, sketched and sculpted
boats on the St. Lawrence River. She is loved by all who have
seen her, and many who have only seen pictures. There is a
mysteriousness about Anna: where did she come from, where
was she built, why was she built, what was she used for in the
Thousand Islands, why is she grounded in Cape Vincent, NY?
The answers to all or most of these questions can be found on
Facebook on a page devoted to her called simply "The Anna," or
a Google search for "the Anna Cape Vincent NY." On the former

you can readily see the devotion people have for her.

I will not recreate those here. You should go there and look at her, if you are in the area and if you have time. I have done my best to add a few paintings and sketches of her to the multitude that exists. People travel long distances just to get a photo of themselves next to Anna. If you do visit her, please be kind. She is located on private property at a marina. Be polite about trespassing. Please understand that too much love and attention can damage her, as she is very old and very fragile.

There are those who say, "preserve her!" and those who say, "no, let her age and make her disappearance normally – leave her be!" I did a full color painting of her in her original painted glory and was told I should not have. People take their love of Anna very seriously. Of course that was only the expressed opinion of one person. While there may be others who feel that way, and want to let her "rest in peace with dignity," there are also those who want to see her fully restored and properly displayed in a protective environment. It's an argument I'll not join. I'm an artist.I don't live there. I shall keep my opinion to myself. Either way, look, don't touch, and above all, do NOT seek souvenirs. She needs no help deteriorating.

The image below is of my favorite of Anna, and can be found on my Fine Art America Website with many others that are not in this book. [https://joel-charles.pixels.com/]

]

Anna in Winter. Grayscale photo of watercolor by author

MORE BOAT ART

The following are random sketches and prints from my boat collection, because I love boats, and drawing them.

Watercolor of Rotary Park on a typical day

Turgeon's Dock as it might have looked in the early 2000's. Grayscale print of black and white watercolor painting from author's photo. The modern boat is in the spot my dad would have moored his Lyman Islander back in the 1950's.

"Convoy" of pleasure craft. Grayscale print of iPencil sketch, from author's photo

"Where old boats go to die", French Creek Marina, Clayton, NY.

"Anywhere", Grayscale print from iPencil painting from author's 2007 photo

The Amundsen, a Canadian icebreaker, Acrylic on 16X24
Canvas, from photo by James R. Miller, with permission.

These ships keep harbors and channels open when the freeze
starts, and in the spring, when the ice is melting and going
out. Canada operates nineteen Coastgaurd icebreakers like the
Amundsen, the US has three. A large part of the Seaway is in
Canadian waters, and all of these ships are busy year round,
even when there is no ice to deal with. We see the distinctively
marked CCG and USCG ships passing even in summer, though
not all of them are icebreakers like this.

Jim Charles' kit built plywood Sunfish. iPhone sketch from author's photo

Judge Ben Wiles tour boat, grayscale image of watercolor, from author's photo. This boat operates on Skaneateles Lake

Long ship passing the "window" formed by Forever Park. It's hard to see in the iPad sketch, but there are sprinklers cooling the deck and the hatch covers and latches. The heat from the sun makes this necessary.

The author's granddaughter at the end of a dock on Lodi Point, Seneca Lake, with sailboat silhouetted in the sunset. Acrylic on canvas from author's photo.

I included information and photos in this chapter to illustrate my love for boats and the St. Lawrence River. Please, if you do buy or rent a boat, be safe. It's a beautiful place to do it, and a grand experience. This is an old boat joke, which I'll repeat here:

Old boat joke

Friend: you know the happiest time in a boat owner's life?

Me: no, what is it?

Friend: When he buys the boat.

You know the second happiest time?

Me: no, what is it? Friend: When he sells it.

Rotary Park Docks on a busy summer day. Watercolor from author's photo

CHURCHES AND CHAPELS

When we came to Clayton, New York from Mooers, New York, we lived for a short time kitty-corner from the Clayton United Methodist Church. In the sixteen years I lived in Clayton with my parents, that was the church we attended. My brothers and I belonged to the Scout troop there, we went to Released Time Religious Education there, and now and then attended church picnics. The latter stopped after I got pushed out of a swing at Cedar Point State Park and my mom decided that, even though my injuries were minor (a small hole in my skull and a concussion) we would not be attending any more church picnics.

But for those sixteen years I was raised as a Methodist. I had no idea at that age as to why that was. It was not until my early 50's, when my brother Jack and I went to Wales together that I found what probably lay behind my Father's Methodist Faith. It turned out that my seven times removed great grandfather, Ciarl Mark (Charles, son of Mark) was a Methodist preacher in Wales, in a little town called Bryncroes. We went to his church, which appears, from the photo in Google Maps, to be a private home now, but was still being used as a church in 1993. We were accompanied by my 7th cousin from the same ancestor,

Beryl Hughes, husband Elwyn and several other more distant relatives. One of them bore a remarkable resemblance to my brother. Our group had just been to the Church of England churchyard in another town where Ciarl Mark is buried.

My grandfather, Oscar Charles, was a 5th generation descendant of Ciarl Mark, from Ciarl's grandson, Owen Charles. The family had emigrated from Wales in the early 1800's to Remsen, New York. My grandfather had left Remsen to become a dentist. Neither he nor my father were particularly interested in telling their descendants about the reason behind their estrangement from the family, so we don't know the why of it, but one can guess. All my ancestors were protestants, Methodist, probably, as that seemed to be the largest denomination represented in Remsen when Jack and I visited there. My dad used to have a saying: A true Protestant is a man who has become disillusioned with his church or his pastor and has left to form a church of his own. As I grew older, I realized the true meaning behind that. Such a falling out may have been the reason. We may never know.

I always liked the church in the little white building on the corner of John and Jane. Even though I became and remain a Catholic these last 41 years, I still enjoyed the tour I got in 2002 when I was in Clayton alone for a week. I had been standing outside, talking with Cordy Reff, who lived across the street next to where I used to live. He saw me taking pictures of the building and came over to talk to me.

Interior of Clayton UMC, much as it looked in 2002

After we had talked for a while, a gentleman came out of the church and saw me talking to Cordy. We spoke a few minutes, then he asked if I would like to see inside the church. We went in and he showed me around. He said it would be alright if I took some pictures, and I did. It had changed little in the 42 years since I had last seen the inside. I somehow have lost the man's name in the 20 years since the tour, but I believe he was a deacon of the church at that time.

Directly across from the Post Office and kitty-corner from the McKinley house is Christ Episcopal Church. Other than to step inside for a brief look to see what it was like, or walk by and take a photo in 2002, I have no memory of ever being inside this church. I've been in many Episcopal Churches since 1960, but never this one for any kind of service. Before that there would have been no reason for me to go inside. It is a sturdy, well designed brick edifice, typical of the Episcopal Churches of the time it was built. It has the second tallest steeple in town and can be seen from the river if you know where to look. I had Episcopalian friends at the time I lived there, but none of us ever discussed religion much when I was growing up, nor attended each other's church. I had no education in the history of the church until I was in college and studied a bit about European history, and the dispute between Henry the

211

Eighth and the Roman Pope regarding the king's penchant for multiple serial wives. It is a beautiful church.

Christ Episcopal Church, John and Hugunin Streets, Clayton.
Freehand ink over pencil sketch from author's 2002 photo

I have to admit that I am not sure if the next church is even a church anymore. It was a Baptist Church when I was growing up, and at some point, became a "community church." I attended a funeral there once, long ago, and have been inside for other reasons – one being the secondhand thrift shop volunteers ran in the basement. A friend and our neighbor at French Creeek Marina, Sandy Thompson, used to volunteer there. It was also used as a Food Bank, but we did not need that service, fortunately. My clearest memory of it was the bus stopping there to drop off other released time students on Wednesdays. At some point I think we may have had released time classes there as young Methodists as well, but the memory is vague. To me it was always that neat white building across from the tennis courts at the opposite end from the Catholic Church on the road that circled the park. Then it was empty. You don't know what you're missing until it's gone.

Former Baptist Church

River Community Church, Freehand ink over pencil, from Google Street View

Once we stopped spending summers in Clayton and became two- or three-week visitor/snowbirds we lost track of a number of things. One was the construction of a new church out on Route 12E at the corner of Bartlett Point Road. I'm not sure of the history, but a neat modern building with a huge lawn is the replacement for the Baptist Church/Community Church. I have not been inside the building, and the photo used for the sketch came straight off Google Street View, but I wanted to include it in the "Churches" section of this book, as it is a contributor to Clayton Life, and an important addition. The church is River Community Church, and sure is a pretty place to worship.

When I was growing up, as a very young child with a super-sized imagination and very gullible, I remember stories about what went on in that huge gray stone building at Mary Street and James. It was always a mystery as to what actually did go on inside, and we protestant children were all convinced that it must be true that they worshipped statues because there was one right out front with a lighted halo! Oh, there was a lot more than that bandied about by those who had no reference point on the matter except what they thought they heard their parents say. As I grew older, I learned from my Religious Ed classes that Catholics did not really worship statues, but that us protestants were forbidden to have 3D or even 2D human likenesses in our churches, and that it was improper to have Jesus 'figure represented on a crucifix, etc. All things that came from the evolution of Protestant churches away from Catholic theology and practice. Things I no longer concern myself with.

As a forty plus year convert, I know that all of that was simply a hangover from the days when comparative religious study was devoutly avoided, and those stories resulted from ignorance. We definitely do not eat babies or drink blood, and we don't worship statues, but we are different in some ways. Aren't we all?

If you had told me in 1950 that I would one day call St. Mary's Church our second home parish, I would have been polite, but disbelieving. Well, we do. It's a long story, and I won't go into it here. It's enough to say that my ancestors would be scandalized were they alive to know that. If you've studied history, you will find that as ironic as I do, since their seven times removed ancestors were either all Roman Catholics or pagan Druids.

At any rate, the church has many memories for me, even from before my time of conversion. All you need do is look at a photo of Clayton from the water and you will see a very important one. You can use the steeple, the tallest one in town, for miles out on the river. Along with Anna and Rock Island Light, St. Mary's is the subject I have most often painted or drawn. Here are a few examples.

St Mary's from across the park. Freehand ink sketch from Author's photo

Freehand grid drawing on canvas as base for acrylic painting by author

(Above) Freehand ink over pencil sketch from author's photo

Freehand ink over pencil sketch from photo by Will D. Curtis

Final Acrylic on 16X20 Canvas by author. Sold. Copies available.

Grayscale print of 16X20 acrylic of St. Mary's on James Street
from photo by author. For Sale. Prints available.

On the grounds of the Clayton Distillery and Chateau Restaurant there is a small chapel that was originally used by the Nuns who lived there when it was called Fairview Manor. When we ate at the Chateau a few years back I took a couple of photos, and these are sketches from them. I'm not sure if it is in use as a Catholic Chapel now, but it is preserved as one. Be sure to walk back and look inside.

Chapel at Fairview Manor/Clayton Spirits/
the Chateau from author's photo

Interior of Chapel at Fairview Manor from author's photo

The Westminster Chapel (Below) stands on a knoll in the woods just outside the community of Westminster, on Wellesley Island. I can't say I have ever seen it, as I was not aware it existed until Kym Peterson-Shackleton posted it on Facebook. I was really taken with the photo. I knew I was going to be doing this chapter for my book soon, and she was kind enough to give me permission to sketch it. I intend to visit one day.

Densmore Baptist Church

There are several small chapels like this scattered around Wellesley and the other islands as well as the mainland. Some are big enough to be classified as churches, and I am reasonably sure, having seen photos of the inside of this one, that it can be and is used for services. One interesting photo shows a tall carved wooden Indian in this chapel where the altar would be.

Originally founded in 1902 as the First Methodist Episcopal Church of Wellesley Island, Densmore is now a Baptist Church, located off Route 100, which runs from one end of Wellesley to the other, Thousand Islands Park to Westminster Park. This beautiful setting has been and is the location of many weddings, concerts and of course, church services. It is a popular spot in the summer.

I photographed the church from several angles one day last Summer when Skeet Bourgeois, Carol and I made our usual pilgrimage to Boldt Castle, with lunch at the Guzzle in Thousand Islands park. I used one of my photos for this sketch and a watercolor painting of the church.

There is no shortage of places to worship in and around Clayton, Alexandria Bay, and surrounding towns and communities. I have always thought of the 1000 Islands as a spiritual place, and I am not alone in that thought. The Community of Thousand Islands Park was originally established in 1875 as the Thousand Island Park Camp Meeting Association, by the Rev. John Ferdinand Dayan. Do a drive through. I think you'll like it.

BACKROADS AND BARNS

For as long as we have been living in or visiting Clayton, and when I was growing up there, I have been watching this barn. It has aged gracefully, but it is now in a state of disrepair that, sadly, is probably beyond fixing. I don't know when it started, but I've been fantasizing about this barn for decades. Last I knew it was still for sale.

The first idea came to me when I was "in theatre" in Tucson. When we went to Clayton from there and I passed this barn I used to indulge in the same pipe-dream as when we passed large vacant buildings for sale or rent "–Wouldn't this make a great theater?" Of course, a rather large infusion of capital would be required, but I could see the potential. Parking for 200 cars, interior shored up and gutted, the interior partition off for dressing rooms and restrooms, an open concept stage built, theatrical lights hung, used theater seats bought and installed, and voila, a community theater.

Along with that daydream I have the skills to do those things, or I did, before I got too old and arthritic to do heavy work. I produced and directed plays, built stages and sets, hung lights and acted on them, in real life, not dreams. So, I knew it could be done. It's like the old joke though. First you have to buy a lottery ticket.

When we left Tucson and moved to Georgia, I took up painting as a hobby. The dream changed. This barn would make a great summer home and studio. Each time we passed this barn the next summer I would think of stopping to photograph it. Finally, I did. And when we went back to Cumming, Georgia after our two-week Clayton fix, I sketched, then painted the barn on canvas. I sold the painting a few years ago to, a Clayton native whose grandfather did the sheet metal work for the ventilators at the top of the barn. I still have the digital copy of the sketch, and I have doodled the barn often since then.

The point is that, along with this barn, I developed a love of painting and sketching barns and old buildings. I paint unused barns mostly, as there is a mystique about old, abandoned barns for me. It goes back to the days of my youth, when my parents used to take me along on back road drives all over Jefferson, Lewis, St. Lawrence and Franklin counties. They loved the countryside, and at least once a week in good weather we would drive somewhere aimlessly. When I took driver training in high school we often drove on back roads, the three or four students taking turns driving for short stretches, until we had to return to school.

Barn on Rt 12, Clayton. Grayscale print of original
pencil sketch on 11X14 Canvas

I got used to driving around the countryside, and in later life Carol and I both continued to do so, wherever we lived. I have barn paintings from Georgia as well. When we were in Clayton, we would do the same. One of our favorite drives was out Rte 12E to Crystal Springs Road. For many years that was also accompanied by a stop at Frontenac Crystal Springs Water company to refill our store-bought gallon water jugs for a quarter and take a look at the "Speakeled Trout", as the original sign used to say. My parents found that hilarious. The sign is no longer there, but the Rainbow Trout are.

Barn on Rt 12, Clayton. Grayscale print of acrylic
painting on 11X14 Canvas (Sold)

The bottled water from this spring, and the company name, were the result of Charles Emery's establishment of the Frontenac Hotel on Round Island. The water emporium was called Frontenac Crystal Springs. The pure spring water was originally for guests of the hotel and the business grew to supply the entire region. There used to be a small hotel and bar operation which was popular as a local watering hole. I may have had a drink or two, or three there myself. The owners were careful about underage drinking though, so I had to wait until I turned 18. That was OK, since I had promised my dad I would wait

until my 18th birthday to try Demon Rum. By the time Carol and I were married, the bar and hotel were gone, and the water company offices occupied the building.

McAvoy Farm, Grayscale copy of acrylic painting on
11X14 canvas board from photo by Art Pundt

That drive usually ended by our turning down French Creek road and returning by Bevins Road, both dirt after the comfort of paved Crystal Springs Road. Right at the Southeast corner was the McAvoy Farm. Mr. McAvoy was a school board member and thus one of my dad's bosses. Mr. McAvoy farmed it until he retired, and Mrs. McAvoy lived on it long after that. Many McAvoy family members would recognize the subject of this painting, viewed from French Creek Road.

There are two stories behind these paintings, done about 4 years apart. The first is from a photo by Art Pundt that I saw on Facebook, posted by Glenda McAvoy. I went to school with Glenda, so I wrote and asked, "May do a painting from the photo?" She approved, and told me the photo artist was Art Pundt, so I called Art and asked permission to paint it. He readily agreed on the condition that I send him a photo of it and give him credit for the photo. I always do that for any photo I use to paint, and most photographers are willing to go along with those conditions. Without thinking, I made the mistake of not doing that once. Once was enough for me to learn that lesson.

McAvoy Farm from Crystal Springs Road. Line sketch on iPad for basis of iPencil painting below, from photo by Rex Hunt, with permissione

McAvoy Farm, iPad painting from photo by Rex Hunt

In one of the few photographs (below) in the body of this book, I am in the process of painting tthe McAvoy farm on my biggest easel, in front of the Scoop. You can't see the painting, but it was the only one I did that summer on 11X14 canvas over hardboard. It's visible from the side in the easel. So is Carol's Nora Roberts novel, which she left with me that morning to go shopping at Rak's, down the street. I never got to read it.

I would be remiss if I did not mention the fact that the McAvoy family and all her friends suffered a great loss with the Passing of Glenda McAvoy. I owe her and Rex Hunt for these last barn paintings. RIP Glenda.

You can see the amount of equipment and supplies I used to need to paint in acrylic. Big tubes of paint, many brushes, and a good-sized easel/paint box. Behind the Easel is the display board I used to use, with 8.5X11 paper prints of my other paintings, in the hope that someone might buy one or two. That never happened. I sell, but not that way.

The artist at work in front of the Scoop

I have this easel in my studio, but Imostly use it for display. I went to an 11.5X18 palette covered in plastic for drawing and water coloring or using my large drafting table when home. It's a lot easier to fly with the palette! I have not done an acrylic painting in two years, except for a 23X29 on paper of balloons from the 2022 Albuquerque Balloon Festival, and an 8X10 on paper of Carol and me watching the Festival Launch of 600 or so balloons.

After we moved to Albuquerque I looked around at the walls of my studio at the 50 plus acrylics I haven't sold (I've sold 12), which take up a lot of space. Right then I decided to go to all watercolor. Now I have gone to a very basic watercolor set and some drawing pads. Did I mention how much easier it is to fly with those? With a few pencils and some styluses, plus the iPad and iPencil, and my laptop, I can paint and store the product in 95 percent less space. Lately I am doing mostly digital, which takes up even less space. I do love looking at my acrylic "children" on the walls though. One day I may sell all of my excess art supplies, but not yet.

The next print is a digital iPencil drawing of a barn I "found" on Black Creek Road in Clayton. My friend Tom Delaney, who used to live nearby on Black Creek Road, advised that this farm belonged to the Aubertine Family. It's not far down the road from where Tom and his family lived, where his father ran a farm just to the north of this one.

I saw this barn and took several photos on one of our Road Trips. It has become something of a habit for me to drive Black Creek Road now, as an annual thing. The photo below it is an ink over pencil sketch of the same barn, from a slightly different angle. As I said before, empty, deteriorating barns are more fun to paint for me than prosperous looking, well painted, occupied barns. There is something tragic about them. These were once just as prosperous as their mates that have not fallen

iPencil painting of Aubertine barn on Black Creek Rd from author's photo

into disrepair and become hidden in foliage. They have a story. I don't always know the story, but I know it is there. It is the same with houses. I'm drawn to (no pun intended) the empty, slightly, or greatly downtrodden ones. They are mysterious, and look like they want to tell me something.

The house below is right across the road from the barns, but I don't have any idea who owns or once owned them last. I believe they may have belonged to the Aubertine family. The history of rural Jefferson, Lewis and St. Lawrence counties is one of ups and downs and changes over the last Century. Just for example, Clayton went from becoming a booming tourist town to a very slow economy, and back again, just since I left there in 1960. The area went from prosperous dairy farming to almost no dairy farms at all in the 21st century. It isn't the purpose of this book to delve into the history of the area and its successes and failures.

What I see may not be what others see. Most of my paintings are of the North Country, specifically the area where I grew up, around Clayton, New York. I now live in New Mexico, an artist's paradise, yet I have yet to draw or paint but four New Mexico scenes. I sit in my studio and think about what I want to do, and go to the computer and find something I remember, and draw, or paint it. It's uncomplicated. No one need interpret my unschooled work. That doesn't stop people from doing it.

House on Black Creek Road. Grayscale print of watercolor
on 8.5X11 sheet, from author's photo

There once was a house, and a barn across the road on our regular route along and across French Creek, which we often took weekly when we summered in Clayton. I can't find my photos of them in all my computer files, so until I do, no sketch. The house burned a few years ago, and I wrote about it.for the Sun. But try as I might, I can't find the article or the photos. So as a result, I can't relate the history of that place. The name of the family that owned it is on the tip of my tongue, but at my age, that's often a very long way from access.

It had been vacant for at least a few decades, but we loved going by and looking at the wide verandah and the Victorian gingerbread, and tall windows, but I never took the time to photograph it. It was a shock to return the summer it burned to the ground and find it gone. The barns were still there. I took photos. Those are the ones I can't find. I would love to do a sketch of that house, and those barns. Opportunities not taken are lost. Maybe one day I will come across photos of them, or someone will find one and give me permission to paint from it.

The shock of not seeing that house, one around which we had woven daydreams like my barn on Route 12, was fully matched by the shock of seeing the sign below as we began our annual trip down memory lane and across French Creek a few years ago. The bridge on French Creek Road was closed!

Bevins Road Bridge closure sign. Just another thing we can't do anymore.
iPencil painting on iPad from author's photo.

We couldn't continue our usual route back up to House Road, and Deferno Road, or Bald Rock Road to Route 12. I took the photo from which I recently did the sketch, and we turned around and went home a different way. One day we will check to see if there is a new bridge, but somehow, I doubt there will be.

Bevins Road. iPencil sketch from my photo from 2011

The photo of Bevins Road below was taken before the French Creek bridge was taken out, probably by high water. Passage along dirt paved French Creek road always took me back to my driver training days, as it was one of the roads we took – probably because of the sharp turn at the top, or the steepness of the narrow road down from House Road and across the creek to Bevins Road. Or just because Coach Allen or Mr. Strouse liked the drive. I will never know. Someone recently bought a copy of it from my Fine Art America site, so it may be we are not the only ones who liked that drive.

One of the ways we love to get to Watertown when we are not in a hurry is to turn right off Route 12 onto County Route 180 at Gunn's Corners. It takes us over through Dexter, and with a few turns, onto Coffeen St. (12F) and into Watertown. There are several barns along this route, but most are back on long driveways on private land, where I do not have permission to go. This brings two things to mind.

Barn on County Route 180. Grayscale print of 8X10 watercolor

First, the traffic on County 180 is not heavy, but it's a 55-mph zone, meaning the occasional 75 is the norm. At this spot there is, like most Jefferson County roads, no good place to pull over and stop. When you do so, you must be very careful to look back before you get out of the driver's side. For this shot, I had Carol drive, and got out the passenger side. It's much safer that way.

Second is the need for another driver, as above. One really should not be staring off the road, looking for good barns to shoot, on narrow, often high-speed county roads. I really would like to get to go home and paint a barn, not If anyone has a photo of a barn they would like to have sketched, or painted (not the exterior, as one wag put it, when he asked if I could paint his barn) please email me a photo, and we can work something out. [jcharlesaz@gmail.com]

Quick watercolor sketch of a familiar barn near
Rte 12E and Crystal Springs Road

Gray Scale print from author's photo

We had to skip Clayton in 2020, because of the pandemic, but we got to there last year. We spent some time with our sister in law Charlene Curtin Green at her place on Bartlett Point.

Zenda Farms barns. Ink over freehand pencil sketch from author's photo

Before we left, knowing that I like painting barns, Charlene suggested a golf cart ride to a spot from which people have rarely photographed the Zenda Farms barns. The following sketch is from that photo shoot. One day I will do a painting from it.

When I was a pre-teen my friend Bryce Baker and I would wander the wooded fields and pastures between the golf course on Rte 12 and East Line Road. I'm sure we were trespassing in many cases, but no one ever seemed to mind. The Railroad crossing at East Line Road was not used as often in the years after 1952, when coal was no longer king on the river. Trains were literally milk trains, with some passengers, and some coal cars, but not the long trains we used to see, and not as often.

Cissy Danforth Nature Trail at Black Creek Road. Freehand
ink over pencil sketch from author's photo

We could go there from the intersection of Black Creek and
Rte 12 at McCarn's Hill, just south of East Line, but we didn't.
When we had, young boys, older and bigger than we, and often
on horseback, always seemed to be around to chase us off.
Names aren't important here. It was long ago. Besides, I have
forgotten them.

Rail trestle on the Cissy Danforth Nature Trail.
Freehand ink over pencil sketch

One day, back in the mists of the pre-teen years, we and the Matthews boys walked the track, across East Line, and all the way to this trestle. They dared me, skinny kid with very weak eyes and bad balance, to walk across the trestle by myself. And come back the same way. It was a time of day there would probably be no trains so, safe right? It turned out to be safe, but who knew. I did it - by myself, as quickly as I could. I had nightmares about it for weeks – never did it again. I probably would have a hard time doing that today. Rheumatoid Arthritis has wreaked havoc on my balance and I'm not sure I could walk that from tie to tie anymore. Fortunately, it seems that there was funding to safety rail the trestle and make it a walking path. It was blocked by a barricade last time i was there, which I am pretty sure kids ignore. It's a challenge, I'm sure, but it is now accessible to cross the creek below. I wish I could, but I can no longer walk that far.

Sometime in 2016 or 2017, our friend Sid (Bud) DeBoer, his wife Gracie, Carol and I were at our usual spot by the river, often referred to jokingly as "the Bench O'Knowledge." We were doing our usual thing, discussing the local, state and world situation, and boats, and the river – while people watching at the same time. Bud knew I was a once a house painter, and now an artist, but he asked me with a straight face how much I charged to paint a barn. I looked at him to see if he was serious – it was hard to tell most of the time – and he seemed to be. He saw my hesitation and jumped in with, "I mean, how much do you get a square foot."

I replied, "Bud, I don't do exteriors anymore." To which he responded, "I know that. I was just kidding. Would you do a painting of my barn?" I agreed, and Gracie sent me a photo she had taken of a large dairy barn. I knew Bud was a dairy farmer but had no Idea how big. When we went home, I started the project, and within a month I had finished a 16X20 inch acrylic of his barn, pictured below. I took it to my printer and had them FedEx it to Bud and Gracie at their home in Pennsylvania. It is one of my favorite barn subjects. I include it here, for its Clayton connection, even though it is a barn in Pennsylvania. Bud was one of my best friends, and I've lost a lot of them over the years. Our last year there before the pandemic he passed away from a long, debilitating illness. We still love seeing Gracie when she can get to the river. It's friends like them we miss when we are not in Clayton.

I have included a few more barn pictures, just because, like boats, I like drawing and painting them. I hope you will enjoy them.

Bud's Barn. Grayscale print of preliminary pencil sketch on 16X20 Canvas.

Typical barn in Northern Georgia – gambrel roof with two side extensions.Grayscale print of 9xX12 watercolor over freehand ink, from Cynthia Charles 'photo

Two more typical Georgia barns. Grayscale print of 9X12 watercolor over freehand ink sketch, From photo by author's professional photographer friend Mike Sussman, who also likes barns.

Mill in Northern Georgia. Grayscale print from watercolor over freehand ink from photo by author's friend, Mike Sussman.

Grayscale print of finished 24X30 acrylic painting of Bud's barn

OUR NEIGHBORS TO
THE NORTH -
A BRIDGE TO CANADA

If you look down river from a boat near round Island, or with binoculars from Frink Park, this is what you will see:

The American Span, 1000 Islands Bridge, watercolor study

It was built across the American Narrows channel, and completed in 1937 for $3,050,000. The dedication was attended by President Franklin Delano Roosevelt and Prime Minister Mackenzie King. Until that point, any traffic into Canada from this part of the United States had to go by car ferry or small boat. It was a historic year, in which the American and Canadian shores were joined by five bridges. The shortest of them carries traffic over the border between Wellesley and Hill Islands. From there, the Canadian spans connect with a Cross Canada highway, Route 401, the Queensway. Many people use the American span to get to summer and year-round homes on Wellesley Island, the second largest in the "1000 Islands." I put that in quotes as there are really 1800 plus "islands," with a strict definition of what the word means. Some, like Wolfe, Wellesley, Howe, Grindstone, Carlton and Murray are quite large, with real communities on them. Others, like Mother-in-Law Island near Boldt Castle, have only one house and a few trees. The islands are split between Canada and the U.S. I don't recall the exact split. That information is probably available somewhere. One Island, Zavikon (two separate islands, actually), is in both Canada and the U.S. You can literally wake up in Canada and walk over a short footbridge to the U.S. The two nations 'flags are usually displayed.

To get to Canada after driving the U.S. span of the 1000 Islands Bridge you must first cross Wellesley Island. You can do so by way of four lane Route 81, which gets you from Pennsylvania to the bridge at Collins Landing, NY or, after crossing the bridge, exiting 81 and following 2 lane County Rte 191. I'd recommend the latter if you have the time, as you get scenery with it, rather than a blur. If you have lots of time, do both – one on the way back from Canada, one on the way to. 191 ends at the customs/toll plaza area on Hill Island.

My brothers Jack and Jim used to serve as deckhands on one

of the boat lines in the late 40's. My favorite story (and I have experienced it) is how the guides used to say "we are now passing through the International Rift between Canada and the United States. If you look closely at the bottom, you can see the border line." There was another one for when they were cruising through the "Needles Eye," a narrow passage between two small islands on the Canadian side of Wellesley: "We are now passing through the Needle's Eye. Notice how close the water is to the shoreline." To this day, tour guides the world over have their little traditional jokes. Of course todays boats are too big for either the rift of the Needle's Eye, so you need to be on a private boat to see them up close. Or if you get out and walk at the international bridge over the rift.

The Toll booth sketch below is from a photo taken several years ago. Interstate 81 continues over the bridge from here. You can buy passes if you are going to be making regular trips or pay a fee that includes passage over the bridges to Canada, after passing through customs. The bridge was closed to all but local Wellesley Island traffic during the Pandemic, as the border with Canada was mostly closed for the last two years. Bridge traffic has gone back to normal now.

The next illustration is of a painting I did from a photo taken by James R. Miller. I saw it posted online and immediately knew I wanted to paint it. I asked James if I might do so, and he gave me permission. He has a way of capturing the river that is sometimes almost mesmerizing. I am not good enough or lucky enough to get this kind of combination - fog, sunset, and a just the right location from which to capture the shot. Someone once told me that the white spot must be an error in the photo. Nope. Sunlight. I have the painting for sale on my web page, but I would be reluctant to part with it, as I like to have it where I can look at it regularly. If it does sell, I will need to have it copied on canvas, so that I can continue to do that.

Sunset at the 1000 Islands bridge in the fog across from Collins Landing.
Grayscale print of Acrylic on 16X20 Canvas. From
photo by James R. Miller, with permission

The next photo is of the sketch I did of the bridge as an ink base for a 9X12 watercolor. The original photograph is by Pamela McDowell, whose photo are often seen in the Thousand Islands Sun. These paintings have special meaning for me. It was under and next to the first tower on the American side, at Collins landing that my father used to take me when he was without a boat; bait and lure casting from this spot, between the shore and the looming concrete base of the American side tower. I never tire of views of this bridge, and the tall towers which support it. Carol and I once walked from the Wellesley

Island side nearly up to the top. We stopped just past the first tower, the one visible in the painting, because Carol realized that the bridge was, as she put it, rocking and rolling. We had been spell bound by the sights of the river below and did not really notice that effect until we stopped. I didn't believe her at first, but when we stopped, and looked up toward the center of the bridge, sure enough – it was rocking and rolling. You can see waves in the bridge deck on a windy day. I should have known right away she was not wrong about the feeling. I had seen movies of a similar bridge, Galloping Gertie, the bridge over the Tacoma, Washington narrows.

100 Islands Bridge from Collins Landing, ink sketch from photo by Pam McDowell, with permission

The bridges were built to do that, at about the same time, and the tension is engineered into their construction. They got it wrong with Gertie, and nearly got it wrong with this span, but corrections were made after Gertie collapsed. It is constantly maintained, and carefully watched. It is also a thing of beauty.

The toll plaza at the U.S. end of the 1000 Islands Bridge.
Grayscale print of 9X12 watercolor

"Blue Moon" over Hill Island, ink sketch from photo
by Karen Millspaugh, with permission

Merrickville is a historic little town on the Rideau Canal, and
a good place to sample Canada. Shops and restaurants and a

"quaint" atmosphere lure thousands of tourists here.

There is a canal lock, and a war of 1812 military garrison blockhouse at the end of the street, just over the canal bridge on St Lawrence Street.

Not far away is another easily accessible lock on the Rideau at Smith Falls, and another at Chafee's Lock, where you will also find a popular old hotel and restaurant, the Opinicon. I went to the latter with my parents 66 years ago, and Carol and I went there 51 years later in 2007, when I took the photos for these drawings. I debated putting the Opinicon in the "Resorts and Hotels" chapter, but it is in Canada, so this seemed like a better fit.

St Lawrence Street in Merrickville. Freehand Ink Sketch, from author's photo

The Opinicon Store, ink sketch from Author's
2007 photo. That's Carol, going in

Back entrance to the Opinicon. Freehand ink sketch from author's 2007 photo.

The street scene below the Opinicon Garden is a view from the front porch dining area of the Kingston Brewery, including the antique vintage delivery van. Over the years we have alternated visiting Kingston, Gananoque, Rockport and Brockville for lunch.

Chafee's Lock. Watercolor over ink sketch from author's 2007 photo

Last time we were there in 2019, the young female officer at the customs kiosk seemed really surprised that we would go to Brockville to have lunch and return the same day.

The Opinicon Garden. Freehand ink sketch from author's 2007 photo

Kingston Brewery, 22 Jansen Ave, Kingston. Watercolor
over ink sketch from author's 2012 photo.

Of course, we have done it every other year up until last year, so
we look at it as a normal thing to do.

KINGSTON, ONTARIO

St. George's Anglican Cathedral. Freehand ink sketch

We like to park and walk around a bit, and this church is one of the things you can see on the way to the Kingston Brewery. One year, accompanied by our friends Carolyn Bourgeois and Sara Norton, we had lunch in Rockport, then drove to Kingston and parked near the waterfront. We walked to one of our favorite places to visit, the old Kingston Rail Terminal, which is now a tourist center and gift shop/museum. There is a Canadian National Railway steam engine parked out back, and shaded areas to sit and watch the waterfront. Across the street is the Kingston City Hall, where you can get a tour of that historic old building.

There is a lot to see and do in Kingston. You can take a streetcar like tour bus and see it in airconditioned comfort, do a walking tour, or just pick some places you want to see and drive to them. There are Lots of places to stay in the area, or you can do as we like to do best - a day trip. There is a "star fort", Old Fort Henry, a relic of the war 1812, and Shoal and Murney Towers. The latter are gun towers commanding the Kingston harbor. No real invasion of Canada ever occurred, but the British feared it would if they did not fortify and garrison vulnerable areas along the river, where such and invasion was feasible.

I have not written much about Gananoque, also a great place to eat, stay and play. There is a casino, if you'd like to spend a little time and money increasing the wealth of the area you're visiting. It is also a pleasant place to walk around. It is omitted only because I have not yet done any sketches from our visits there.

As this is a narrative wrapped around my sketches and not a tourist guide or history book, I will leave to you the fun of researching what you might like to do in this easily accessible area of Canada. You will find Canadians a welcoming and pleasant lot, and I highly recommend visiting. I do hope you are able to visit Canada. Many of the people living in and visiting Clayton have roots across the river. It has traditionally been one of the most open and friendly borders in the world, and I hope it stays that way.

Kingston Rail Station. Grayscale print of Acrylic on
16X20 canvas. From author's 2018 photo

DOWN BY THE RIVER - SUNSETS

Nearly every day we are in Clayton we end up down by the river, either at Frink Park, or at Rotary Park. Sometimes there is just too much going on at Frink Park, such as a band concert or singing group. As younger people we would have enjoyed those, but at our age it just seems that anything too loud for conversation is not an activity we crave. But normally, after a light supper, we get in the car and head for the river. We used to walk, but age has caught up with us, and we're just too slow. If we're lucky we'll find a spot park. You don't have to put money in the meter after 6 PM, and we're rarely there before 7, and gone by 9:30 or 10.

Our favorite pastime, if no one is around to chat with, is watching the leisurely progressions of ships passing, sometimes actually passing each other, up and down-bound, and the often near frenetic pace of the smaller craft, going about the business of fishing, carrying passengers, or just sightseeing. I'm not alone in enjoying the view of the Clayton Waterfront, and it is best enjoyed from a boat. The variety of boats adds to the entertainment provided by a St. Lawrence Sunset. There are not many places like it. I'll try to describe one here.

Freehand ink sketch of a down-bound freighter

First, the sun lowers over the top of Grindstone Island. Depending on how far into the summer season you are, the placement of the final departure of the sun from view varies. Early in the year it will disappear behind the head of Grindstone, gradually moving to the northwest, and at the longest day of the summer it will set behind Calumet Island if you are observing it from Rotary or Frink Park. I have not seen a winter sunset in 62 years, so I can't tell you much about one. As the summer progresses, the sunset will be behind Governor's Island, and there will be a reversal of its path, until it is finally setting as far west as you will see it. Because Clayton is relatively far north, that sunset will be far later than it is in, for example, Arizona. And it will be noticeably later than Elmira, NY. From early June to late July the sky will be lit up with the afterglow until nearly 10PM. I can not even begin to describe the colors. You need to see them, or look at 1000 Island River Rats or the sites on Facebook or in Chamber of Commerce literature. Better yet, go there and see for yourself.

Self Unloader upbound in the sunset, quick freehand Ink Sketch

As anywhere else from where you may be watching a sunset, sky conditions will vary the visual effect. While cloudy skies may herald bad weather, they make for far more interesting sunsets than clear blue skies. The topography of the land, the presence of the river and the lakes to the west all lead to high moisture content in the air, and quite often large cumulous clouds form north and west of the river, in Canada. These tend to generate the most spectacular sunsets, particularly when there are high cirrus clouds over the Canadian shore overlaying the view of the tall cumulous towers behind them.

Long streamers of cirrus clouds by themselves also make for gorgeous sunsets, particularly if there are masses of cumulous clouds on the far horizon in Canada, instead of a few dozen miles north of the border.

Tall Ship downbound, freehand ink sketch from
photo by Dan Blank, with permission

It's the variety that surprises. On an extremely cloudy evening there may be little evidence of a sunset at all, except for a big red orange ball barely visible through the low clouds. The sunsets in summer are quite slow, comparably, and can provide entertainment and awe for an hour or more. They usually start around 7:30 or 8PM, and last until 8:30 to 9:30, depending on the time of year. Photographers - be sure to linger until the end, because the sunset you just made a shot of may not be the best moment. It's worth the wait.

The best time for sunset photos may sneak up on you, if you are not watching closely. And one important thing to remember is that the time to catch a sunset's best in a photo is right before it goes down. At that point the light from the sun is coming over the "edge" of the Earth as it rotates away from the sun, West to East. That means that instead of burning through the clouds between you and a higher sun, it is hitting and reflecting off the bottoms of the clouds, illuminating them with color from reflected light, rather than refracted light. That may not be scientifically accurate, but it's the timing that is important. Just when you thought it was over, it gets better. Depending on atmospheric conditions – dust, smoke, pollen, or other particulate matter in the air or contained in the water droplets that make up clouds, the color will vary from light yellow to dark red orange. My favorite, which I seem to rarely catch on film, is when there is a band of blue sky between the clouds in the distance and the nearer clouds. That band may appear to be a greenish blue, almost turquoise. The sky is almost never that color except at sunset. The variety of sunset colors is often surprising, and even if you are not a photographer, St. Lawrence sunsets rarely disappoint.

The following scenes are of different locations for viewing sunsets. One of my favorite spots when we were not down by the river was from our screened deck at French Creek Marina. We could see the sun set next to the St. Mary's Church spire. Of course there were the marina work and storage buildings in the way, so if we wanted a cleaner view we could walk one of the campground roads and view sunsets from there. One spectacular view is through the space under the French Creek bridge.

Creek Sunset", Acrylic painting from a photo by Dan Blank, with permission

The only unobstructed view of a sunset is, of from space. The obstruction of clouds and the horizon are what make good ones down here on Earth.

Sunset over calumet from dock level. Watercolor
by author from Will Curtis photo

View from Rotary park at sunset, Watercolor from author's photo

Tourists, just disembarked from a 1000 Islands tour at Frink
Park, acrylic on 20x24 canvas from author's photo

DOWN BY THE RIVER
– ACTIVITIES

Clayton is a bike friendly town. There are hills, but they're not too steep. It's a good way to see the village, without worrying about where to park your car, or meter money. The sketch below shows a bike parked along the river walk, before the Marina was built. The path is still there, now paved with brick, and still bike friendly, but be careful of pedestrians. They'll be found enjoying the path as well.

Ink sketch from author's photo, before the marina was added. Little Round and Round Island, the 1000 Islands bridge, and the Northwestern end of Washington Island can be seen in the background

Sitting is a great thing to do by the river. Not far from where the reference photo for the digital painting of the Adirondack chairs was shot, you can find these comfortable chairs to rest in, watch boats go by or just enjoy the view and the people passing by.

Frink Park Pavilion, iPad painting from author's photo.

There will be opportunities to get out on the river, on a tour boat, in a friend's boat or one you rented or brought with you. But you shouldn't miss this one. In the shed pictured below are You'll also find them used as Adirondack guide boats. The boat is pointed at both bow and stern. It comes in many sizes large and small enough to be rowed by one or two people. A side mount can accommodate a small trolling motor. They resemble a large, planked and ribbed canoe. They can be smooth sided or lapstraked. Most I've seen have been the latter. You can rent one here, at the Antique Boat Museum, and take it out into French Creek Bay, and up French Creek if you can row that far. They are easy to row and handle well. They were often used as fishing guide boats, and the oarlocks are positioned so that one person can row and one or more person fish. The museum has a boatwright shop that gives boatbuilding lessons, and you may see how a skiff is built. While you are there you can also view the extensive collection of boats and marine engine displays. As you can guess from the museum's name, nearly all the boats classify as antiques. There are also boat shows, poker runs, and just the occasional sight of a large boat being moved.

I mentioned in an earlier chapter that the center of Riverside drive, from John to James, is occasionally used for auto shows and boat shows. The latter are not connected directly to the boat museum but are part of Clayton being right on the river.

The Antique Boat show at the Antique Museum, across the lagoon from the Boat House. Grayscale print of 12X24 acrylic on canvas

The next sketch is of the harbor/lagoon where ships used to be built. It is also the home of the Antique Boat Museum. The viewpoint is the dock where the speedboats are moored. If you don't do anything else along or on the river, do this. You get to ride in a classic reproduction of a Hacker Craft triple cockpit speedboat driven by an expert pilot, and see enough of the river and the landscape around it to make you want to come back for more, maybe a lot more. People fall in love with this river. It is hard to leave it when the time comes. Ride in the back. Get a little wet. Fantasize that you are a guest at one of the big river homes or hotels and the owner has taken you for your first speedboat ride. Or imagine you own the boat, and the others aboard are your guests. Or go even further – it's your big house and Hacker runabout. Just enjoy.

where

Hacker Craft Speed boat used for tour rides, from author's photo

You may love Alexandria Bay, where there is a carnival like atmosphere and fun to be had all day, but the town is often busy, with an influx of tourists and people participating in shows. There is an annual Poker Run, in normal times, when there is the roar of powerful boat engines running the course from Alex Bay to Clayton and back, or vice versa. Sometimes Clayton has the honors of hosting.

It isn't one of my things, so I am not familiar with it, and we have never been in Clayton for a car show, so I can't describe either one with much accuracy, but they are popular. If you get your hands on a copy of the 1000 Islands Sun, you can see the schedule for the many events for the area.

Watercolor from Jason Desjardines' aerial photo of Downtown Clayton on a quiet summer day. Believe me, it's not always this quiet.

Then there are the standard tourist things to do. Riverside drive and James Street are the main commercial thoroughfares in Clayton, and you will find shops open nearly every day, from at least 9 to 5, sometimes later. You can have a wine tasting at Coyote Moon, then go next door to Hilda's Ladies shop, visit Reinman's home decorating store on the other side, or cross the street to the Eagle Shoppe. If You're an American Legion member you can stop in for a cold beverage and drink it at the bar with fellow Legionnaires or sit by the back window in air-conditioned comfort, watching the boats go by. There are cafes, restaurants and clothing stores enough to browse through, and Michael Ringer's art gallery on the corner of James and Riverside. Or you can find a quiet spot to sit and just watch the river, people, boats, or just read or paint, as I do. There is a reason Clayton was voted the number one small town to visit by USA Today. That's because it is.

ENTERTAINMENT

There is one, sometimes two outdoor concerts at Frink Park weekly. The above sketch was made from a photo shot before the new pavilion. If music outdoors doesn't strike your fancy, there is nearly always something going on at the Clayton Opera House. Plays, bands, comedians, dancers; it may be happening while you are there. The Opera House was built in the 1800s and has a long history. The

Concert by the River at Frink Park. Freehand ink Sketch from author's photo
Opera House Community Orchestra concert. Ink sketch from author's photo.

tower on the top once held a clock, the outer face of which

Clayton Community Orchestra performs at the Opera house. Ink sketch from the author's photo.

now adorns the building front next to Rotary Park, where Freighters and DiPrinzio's are located. The tower was used during WWII as an aircraft spotting location manned by civilians. The stage, much to my thespian side's delight, is raked a few degrees as was traditional when it was built. The rake, tilted toward the audience, helps lighting and acoustics, and some would say it forces the actors downstage, more toward the audience and into the lights, to be better heard and seen. As a boy I was in a Scout troop sponsored by the Methodist Church, and we met at the Opera House. We had free rein over the first floor where the audience sits. The floor also served as a basketball court, with the basket hung over the stage. When we broke into small groups some of us would meet upstairs in the balcony, where the floor is stepped for seating. The current (I believe) theater office was the local Radio Club's meeting room, and those of us studying Morse Code could meet in there, under supervision. Hands off the equipment.

Clayton Opera House, ink sketch from author's photo.

Carol and I ushered shows for a couple of summers when we lived in Clayton and got to see all the shows free. The building sat mostly idle for many years, except for the period it was occupied by Pruzon's dry goods store and a small restaurant in the basement, under the stairs, and the Masonic Hall on the third floor. The village offices were located there after the businesses closed, and the Thousand Islands Museum as well, until the latter two found homes elsewhere before the Opera

House was remodeled and returned to its original function.

Of course it music and dancing are your preference, there are other venues, like O'Briens, and occasionally the Resort, or in fact, many other places. You'll find it all listed in the pages of the Thousand Islands Sun.

CLAYTON STREET SCENES

These sketches are of only a few of the shops, eateries, and sights along Clayton Streets. I wish I could include everything, but there is so much to see, and observe. These are just typical sights, and my limited sketches of them.

Reinman's Decorating, Coyote Moon and Hildas, typical shops on Riverside Drive. Freehand ink sketch from author's photo.

Clayton Trading Company (Left) and The Thousand Islands Museum.
Grayscale print from iPad painting based on author's photo

Visit the little Bookstore on Riverside Drive (little house on the right in above photo) and peruse the books by local and other authors. Many are about the river, or have the river as a backdrop to the plot. It is on one of the two "little houses" that were moved to Riverside Drive.

Walking riding a bicycle, or driving, the streets of Clayton are quite beautiful in spring in summer, with few hills, and lots of level walking on well maintained sidewalks. Now that the Utility Line project is done on James and Riverside, there are few construction zones. The trees, except for the lower end of James and along Riverside Drive, overarch the sidewalks, so it can be a pleasant, shady

Jane Street Garden, Watercolor from author's photo

Yost's Garden, 2020, original freehand ink sketch from
artist's photo, used as base for watercolor

walk or ride. Many people have gardens, but my favorite is this one along Jane Street at Webb. The ones pictured ar from photos years years apart, as well as the digital drawing below of the same garden in a different year.

This house on Beecher Street pictured below the garden photos is the first home I remember, from four years old to 10 or 11. It now belongs to our friend, Pia Hogue. In 2021 she welcomed us to her home to see how it had changed.

Garden on Jane Street. Grayscale print of iPad
painting from author's 2003 photo

She has done some remodeling and redecorating but kept the
basic features mostly the same. The back porch is updated, but
I still recognized it as the place I spent many hours, lying on
an old wooden sofa, exercising my lazy left eye, with a patch
over the right eye, or recovering from one of my many bouts
with one respiratory problem or another. There was a sandbox
on the south side of the porch, next to the walk that runs back
from the street on that side. Bryce Baker and I used to build
sandcastles in it, and roads to run our toy cars on. When I
was first wore them I didn't like them, even though I could see
better with them. Introduced to glasses at around two and a
half,

Beecher Street. Ink Sketch from author's photo

I used to lose them in the sand of that box, as even seeing better in them did not make me like them. My father saw to it that I quickly got over that.

Growing up in that house has many good memories. My grandma used to come and visit, sometimes staying for weeks. When we moved to Graves Street, she finally came to live with us permanently, moving into a room on the first floor, to which my parents added a half bath.

737 Graves Street

We moved to Graves Street in 1952, shortly before my mother received an inheritance from a spinster aunt, as did her mother, my grandma. It was a sizable sum for those days, and it allowed my parents to move up a notch, becoming homeowners instead of renters. The house, was upgraded and remodeled, including a new oil furnace, which replaced the huge coal burning octopus in the cellar. No more ashes to be hauled out. Puff back from the oil burner was a different story altogether. When I became an insurance adjuster, I had personal experience in dealing with them. Messy things – coating every cobweb in the house, much to my mother's chagrin.

I remember taking off from the ice on French Creek bay in a yellow canvas skinned Piper Cub, which I think was piloted by Don Gray, and seeing this house from the air, with sheets drying on the line in the very cold air.

My first pet, Rusty, tried to capture a six- foot rat snake in the chicken manure pile next to the coop in the yard next door. Mr. Tiffany, who lived across the street, owned that lot. He once kept chickens, but had not in many years when we moved in. There was a short period when he allowed some of us to use the coop like a club house, but a couple of the older boys were smoking in there one day, and he caught them. A padlock was installed. There's always somebody or something to spoil a good thing. I could, I think, write a whole chapter on this house. But that is not the subject of this book.

The next sketch is of a house I remember quite well, as my friend Becky Marshall used to spend a lot of time there.

She called it her "Cookie Grandma's" house. The sketch was preliminary work for a painting I did for her. My friend Jim Marshal lived one street east, in a house in front of the tall water standpipe that supplied the town. Both houses are still there today, very much changed, but no standpipe. It has been replaced by a municipal garage. There was a large Elm tree at the left of the house, and it too is gone now. Probably passed from old age, as It was quite large, thus old, when we lived there. Or maybe the Dutch Elm Beetle got it in the 1960's.

Cookie Grandma's House. Becky Marshall's Grandma lived here.
Pencil sketch on canvas from Becky Marshal's photo

The sketch of the Clayton sign, looking down James Street toward the river, is as it looks today. This is the third iteration of the sign, in nearly the same place, since I was a child. This intersection holds many memories for me. To the right is a gas station which was Gerald "Gerry" Hammond's place of business then. I used to use his free air to blow up my bike tires. Sometimes I would hang around (too long probably) to watch what went on in the two repair bays or the office adjacent. When I was at Syracuse University, I ended up working for nearly two years at a nearly identical Arco station in East Syracuse. I was right at home.

To the left was the Gayhead Corner Market, or Bogenshutz's store, later operated by Burt Patterson and his wife His wife Rae Hammond, Gerry's daughter. It has not been operated as a store for quite some time, but that is still the way I remember it. One day something else will be there, as is the way with Clayton.

You can't see it in the sketch, but just north of the other corner there was a sporting goods store (now a 2 car garage) run by Ozzy Steel. He used to get a charge out of ribbing me about the BB shot I bought there, referring to me as "Joel the mighty hunter," or something like that. I used my Daisy Air Rifle for target shooting. It must have done some good, because I qualified as an expert rifleman in Army Basic Training.

I have sat waiting at that James and State traffic light for many hours over the last 80 years. I can't drive through there without a memory surfacing.

The next sketch is of Lower James Street, from in front of the Thousand Islands Museum, from a photo I took a couple of years ago. One thing that's immediately obvious is the presence of power poles and lines. I was once told that an artist should leave things out of a painting that detract from it. I would assume the person meant that to include sketches as well. I incorporate or I don't. Mostly I do in sketches. I sketch what I see, and I could leave things out, but choose not to. Paintings are different. It depends on the piece, and what I am thinking at the time. It's mostly exactly what I see, as I see it.

It is not obvious, but this photo is pre street improvement, and the area where the power lines have been removed is not clearly visible in the scene. I'm one of those who feels Clayton would be even more beautiful without the power lines and am happy with what has been done downtown.

Lower James Street, looking North, from author's photo

The area in the photo has many memories for me. Doctor's office on the right, Calzada's Town and Country Restaurant just past the building where the 1000 Island Museum is now, the Bertrand Hotel, Graves Drugs, and the Bertrand Theate r, now Lyric Coffee House. My friend Jim Marshall worked at Calzada's,

The sketch below with the lighthouse in the center background is lower John Street. The river and Calumet Island are behind the lighthouse. Not visible on the right is Reinman's Hardware and directly across the street RAK's is visible. Reinmans has been Reinman's as long as I can recall, in one form or another.

Lower John Street, at Riverside Drive, from author's photo

I remember when Reinman's was a news, tobacco and sundries shop. My brother Dick worked there in the 50's until he turned 18 and started tending bar at McCormick's. One of his favorite perks at Reinman's was getting the Sporting News before everybody else. He was a big Cincinnati Reds, and baseball overall fan. He used to hold one of my drum sticks like a mic and do sports announcer type recaps of games, statistics and all. RAK's used to be Nunn's Appliances, and the Christmas Store to the left on the river side of Riverside drive was Hungerford Hardware. The sketch below with the stop sign is from Will Curtis beautiful photo of John and Riverside Drive. Reinman's is at the right. I did a watercolor from this sketch.

John and Riverside Drive, from a photo by Will Curtis

The sketch from in front of the Eagle Shoppe below shows Riverside Drive, looking East, near the front of what used to be Streets Insurance office. I left out any power lines, but there is a power pole in the distance, Between the Christmas Shop and Rak's, in front of Memorial Park. Right next door to Streets was Merle Daley's Smoke shop, where the paperboys gathered on the sidewalk to roll and fold the Watertown Daily Times before delivery. My throw was pretty accurate, as it was harder for me to dismount my bike and get the paper out from under a bush than it was to throw it where it belonged, so I learned how quickly. If it wasn't a sport depending on strength or decent peripheral vision of things that moved at me left or right, I was good at it.

The westward view of Riverside Drive is also pre pole removal, and I left out most poles and wires. This is the way I remember it for most of the last 60 years. The trees, of course, are gone; there are new ones awaiting time to grow. I am not at all sad that it does not look like this anymore. They will grow, and the beauty added by the subtraction of power lines will remain.

RIVERSIDE Drive

Riverside Drive looking East, from author's photo

The moonbeams drawn in the next sketch don't do the Will Curtis photo justice. I did a watercolor that approached what is there in the original, but it's still not as dreamlike as Will's shot. It is of lower Merrick St. with the he Opera House is on the left, the Popcorn Store and Atillio's Pizza straight ahead, with the old "Herald House"/Thousand Islands Inn on the right. Just visible behind the latter, across Riverside Drive next to Atillio's, is Brian Lesner's studio. He does the same kind of subjects I do, only he's far better at it! To the left is what is now the Pocorn store. The gray scale print below of a water color from a photo by Will Curtis is the River Rat Cheese store, right next door to the Lyric Café. We love sharp cheese, and we usually get some Unfortunately, we forgot this year, 2022.

Ink sketch of lower Merrick Street at night, from Will Curtis' photo

River Rat Chees, Grayscale print of 9x12 watercolor
from photo by Will Curtis

The sketch of the American Legion Hall is from a screen shot, cropped from Google Street View, since I did not have my own photo. I've been a Legion Member since 1971 but transferred my membership to the Colon Couch post in the early 20's, when we lived in Clayton. We don't get in there much anymore, as I am not active in Legion affairs, and can no longer drink.

The American Legion building

But we love to sit by the big back windows and watch the river when we do stop in. There is always activity out there, even at night. And there are always locals socializing in the bar area. My medical aversion to alchohol doesn't keep me from buying a beer or two for Carol and others.

The line sketch below is from a Will Curtis photo of a friend enjoying the fishing off the Clayton River Walk. Somewhere I have a photo I shot of a fisherman with a good sized pike he caught doing just this. It reminded me of the record pike my dad caught just downriver from here, casting off the coal dock.

My friend Don Lingenfeltei calls what I do "Scribble Art," but added that he likes it. I do detailed drawings sometimes, as seen above, but my favorite thing is the quick sketch, using simple lines, and yes, scribbles. My thought is, if you can recognize it, I've done it correctly. It's probably the lack of formal art training on my part.

Fishin', from a photo by Will Curtis

One of those "detailed drawings" mentioned above is one I did of the old wood benches at Rotary Park, before the plastic ones replaced them. This actually started life as a ligh tracing, not much detail, of my photo from this angle. I sometimes use a light box for that, and do a transfer to a piece of art paper or canvas to be sure I have the placement and proportions right for a painting. This is a drawing on top of that, which I later finished with watercolors. I include it here because in my childhood these were the benches that were here at sidewalk level. The photo was taken in 2002, and at some point those benches were replaced with new dark brown plastic benches. I think the new ones are more comfortable

Riverside Drive, Rotary Park side. The Golden
Anchor is in the right background.

People Love to pose next to, in front of, behind and yes – even on the anchor at Frink Park. Along with the official sign (now with miniature Frink Snowplow attached) this symbolizes Frink Park. Much has happened and continues to happen here. It could be said that, with these things and the magnificent faux rail station pavilion, much of Clayton's history is represented in this one spot.

Ship's anchor in Frink Park at the end of Webb Street, from my photo

Below is a hastily drawn sketch of the view from a bench at the Pavilion this July, no photo involved. I now wish I had taken more time with it, as the leaping Muskie statue by Will Salisbury is only barely recognizable just right of center. Will passed away shortly after we left Clayton this year. His contributions to North Country art, and his magnificent personality will be missed. RIP, Will. You live on in your art.

West end of Frink Park. Brian Lesner's studio,
and Will Salisbury's Muskellunge Statue

The other end of Riverside drive, Bella's on the
right. ink sketch from author's photo

I say Clayton is represented well in this park because -if you know what you are looking at - the memories of shipbuilding, the coal fueling dock, passenger liners mooring here, band concerts, "Punkin 'Chunkin'" contests, Parades, boat exhibits, weddings, photo shoots, the now gone Frink Snowplow Plant (still visible in the 2002 sketch of the anchor) and the occasional record fish are all suggested when you look around. One of the reasons for this book is to help you be aware of what you are looking at. Clayton has been described in many ways, one of which is "quaint little town." It is that, but it is ever so much more, and a great place to live. When you visit, you will see what I mean. Don't take my word for it. Come and see for yourself.

OUT ON THE RIVER

Right up to now you may or may not have learned a lot about the river, and Clayton. But you could visit Clayton, or even live there, and never or very rarely experience the reality of the river, up close and personal, to use a cliché. I can not imagine doing so, but it is possible. I have told you a few things you need to know, but some things, important things, you need to learn for yourself.

I know people or have known people who have lived on the river for all or most of their lives, and people who moved to Clayton, for whatever reason, to live here permanently. They are affectionately known as River Rats. Many, if not most of them, make their living on it or from it. I've been told unless you grew up, and still live here, and have done some wild and crazy things on the river, you don't know it well and are not truly a "River Rat." I've heard stories of things I never experienced, because I never needed to as an adult, and couldn't as a boy because I was too sickly until I reached my teens. By then I was not an adventurous sort, and truthfully, I am still not.

Oh, I've fallen through the ice on ponds and at the edge of the river, but I never went out far enough to end up more than waist deep in the freezing water. I've waded knee deep in ice cold to warm pond water at the Clayton Golf Course looking for shagged balls in the muck at the bottom. But I did not put my face in the fertilizer laden water to look for them. I did not learn to swim until I left Clayton, and that kept me away from deep water unless I was in a boat. I did a lot of that - boating, but I've been told, more than once, that I'll never be a river rat officially unless I've done some of those often necessary and dangerous things. I still consider myself one, and truthfully it makes little difference. I've known and heard about some heroic exploits out there. But I'm never going to be able to tell my grandkids that I did anything remotely heroic. That wasn't my experience, and it probably is never going to be the average reader's experience. If it's OK with you folks, I'll continue to think of myself as a "River Rat."

It's not my place to tell someone else's tales, so I will leave it that I know they are not exaggerating. At least not much. They really did swim three miles to shore towing a boat out of gas. They really did nearly freeze to death after falling through the ice in an open lead. I will let them tell you, if they are so inclined. Most I've found to be rather taciturn about those things, so you probably shouldn't ask. Let them volunteer it.

It's safe to say that, unless you know what to do, or learn quickly what needs to be done in a bad situation, the river can kill or maim you. Again, I won't give details about how I know that – just accept that I do.

I have seen people come to the river and express awe at its size, power, and beauty. Often, if they are not discerning people, they will lose track of the reality of the first two in observance of the last. On rare occasion that kills them. Experienced river folk are contemptuous of "rental captains," I'll call them, who come to the river and rent or bring power boats they are ill equipped to manage safely. Not all such rental clients are like that. Yours truly is one exception. I grew up on the river, learned about boat handling (sometimes the hard way) and I acquire, read and understand charts. I also know that I am too old and feeble in the balance department to captain a boat. Some "rental captains" are not renters at all, but own their own boats, trailer them in for a couple of weeks, running them about as though they think they own the river. Occasionally they get owned by the river. I've seen the result of this firsthand, as I used to be an insurance adjuster with a company that sold a lot of marine and personal liability insurance.

Hitting a shoal, a rock or just shallow water at full throttle can be fatal. Thankfully it usually isn't, but it can be. Most often the result is a holed hull, or a sheared pin (that pin that keeps your prop from free spinning on its shaft), or worse, an expensive prop battered to destruction. All the latter things are not fatal but can ruin your day. The fatal thing can ruin your life. That's not what coming to the river is about. Be safe.

Also, be courteous. If you do rent or trail your own or borrowed boat to the river, dont be "that guy." Know and obey the rules of the road. Always watch where you're going. Have a spotter, but remember, you're the captain, and the responsibility is all yours. You could run over a swimmer, a skier, a diver, or cut someone's fishing line. You could anchor in a spot where signs clearly tell you there are underwater power and phone lines, and you shouldn't anchor there. Those lines are hard to repair or replace. Or you could be going too fast in a no wake zone, damaging the docks and the boats moored to them as you pass. Don't be that guy, the one people are shaking their fists or giving you a one finger salute as you pass, instead of giving you a friendly wave. You can have fun without being a dangerous jerk. People come here to have fun, or relax, or work. Don't have fun at someone else's expense.

That said, the river can also be the greatest place to do what we humans call recreation. The possibilities are only limited by your imagination. There are castles and estates and humble cottages that are surrounded by water on all sides; the changing colors of the water; iridescent wave patterns sparkling in the sun; myriad boats and birds and sometimes beasts going about their daily existence; sunrises and sunsets that are the equal of any world-wide, and often better; air that has been described in hyperbole since tourists began coming here. You have to experience the river's many moods to believe them.

Come at the right time in Winter and you will see the river frozen from shore to shore, ice thick enough to drive a car on, move a house from Island to island, hold horse races on, or "just" do a daily commute from Grindstone or another island. If the conditions are right, bring your snowmobile, as there are lots of trails that welcome them. Be careful on the ice, though, if you don't know the river well, and remember, snowmobile trails depend on the good will of the landowner whose fence you decide to breech.

Come in the Fall and see the bright yellow, orange, and red leaf display spread across the islands and on the shore. I recall working at McCormick's, when tourists by the busload arrived and disembarked hungry after a long

Devil's Oven ink sketch from composite of memory and photos

ride to see the Fall Color show from God's paintbrush. McCormick's is gone but they still come. Watch the Punkin' Chunkin 'contest as those orange gourds get hurled by catapult and trebuchet out into the mighty St. Lawrence.

Come in the spring and see and hear the ice go out. Watch as the arrival of spring seems to pop leaves from the trees, quickly turning the streets into canopied by- ways that last all summer into the fall. Expect spring to be much later up here though, as this is a lot higher latitude than southern New York or, even more, Georgia. You may even arrive at the time the Sea Way is opened, and the big colorful buoys that sat all Winter on the dock at Frink Park get put back in to mark the channel. You may see some of the earliest transits of freighters up or down, sometimes through a channel just recently visited by an icebreaker you got to see working.

And Summer. That's the star of the show. That's when you can actually get out on the river and see what all the excitement is about. I have included some sketches below, from my and others 'photos, to illustrate what you might see from a boat, whether it be yours, Uncle Sam's, or your friend Chris'. That's when you can experience sitting by the river, quietly watching the boats go by, and catch some of those magnificent St. Lawrence sunsets, or if you are an early riser, sunrises.

Atillios's Pizza and the Clayton Popcorn Co. from the river

You can catch the impressive 4th of July fireworks display (often on the 3rd or 5th), a band concert on the riverside, grab an ice cream in a fresh made waffle cone at the Scoop and enjoy a conversation, or just people watch at Frink Park. I wish I could be there with you.

If you start your journey from a Clayton mooring or dock, one of the first things you'll see is the Clayton waterfront. I've heard it described by degrees ranging from ugly to beautiful. Beauty is in the eye of the beholder, they say, and I behold it as beautiful. Whatever the architecture, waterfront buildings everywhere show their utilitarian sides unashamedly. Most of Clayton's riverside buildings have balconies or porches, some enclosed, overlooking the water. They are probably the best views in town. Regardless of your opinion, this particular waterfront is unique to the 1000 Islands. Cape Vincent and Alexandria Bay don't have a contiguous row of buildings right on the riverbank like this. From out on the water, you can see much more than the buildings that line it. The grayscale image of my painting below includes things behind the buildings - the appearance of a forest, which is the trees lining all the streets. The ones in front, directly behind the buildings on Riverside Drive are all gone now, replaced by saplings that will grow to look like this one day.

Also visible is the spire of St. Mary's, a landmark that can be seen and followed from afar. The St. Lawrence is a large body of water, and you would be surprised how quickly you can become disoriented out there with no landmarks.

If you pass by Frink Park, you might see one of the concerts pictured in this photo in summer. The sketch below is from a photo taken before the Pavilion was built. I have never done so, but I have wondered what a band concert or choral group would sound like if listened to from a boat in front of the park. They say sound carries across the water, and I have seen (heard) that to be true. But how, I wonder, does music fare over water? Since I became profoundly deaf a few decades back, I'll likely never know, because concerts do not sound like much but noise to me now, even with high quality hearing aids.

Clayton Waterfront, grayscale print of 12X24 acrylic painting by author from memory and a composite of many photos.

The photo after the band concert is of the lagoon nestled between the Antique Boat Museum and the curve of Riverside Drive after it leaves "Downtown." The shore side of Riverside Drive is populated with boathouses and homes, one of which is a home above a boathouse, which belongs to friends, and where we rented a couple of summers. It's and experience we'll never forget, being right on the water, hearing the wave lap the pilings, watching hundreds of boats moving around in the bay/lagoon, and of course the Osprey's nesting at the top of the light on the Boat Museum pier. Chris Muggleton has taken us on boat rides from there, as has his brother-in-law, Joe. It's

Concert at Frink Park, ca 2005, from author's photo

Riverside Drive from the bay or lagoon in Clayton. The
Boat House is the building directly
under the lowest point of the cloud. Ink sketch from author's photo

like being part of the river. You can see the Boat House in
the center of the photo. The sketch of the speedboat was made
from a photo I took either just before or just after our tour on
it. I put this sketch in a second time because this is one way you
can inexpensively and safely go "out on the river." It's a great
ride, with an experienced, licensed captain, who takes the time

to tell you what you are seeing, as any good guide would. Neither Carol nor I can easily get into a speedboat anymore, but they do help if you need it. I highly recommend it as high on a list of things to do on the river. If you buy a museum membership, I believe one ride is either free or reduced cost.

Speedboat ride at the Antique Boat Museum from author's photo

The second photo below is of a Great Blue Heron posing on the shore of the Cut between Murray Isle and Wellesley Island. I took the photo on which it was based while we were on the speedboat tour.

That is another thing you can enjoy while out there. You may even see Osprey, Cormorants, tons of Seagulls and Terns, Loons, many species of ducks, Swans, even Eagles. People have been known to see foxes, deer and other animals swimming between islands as well. There is always something to see, like the Great Blue Heron below.

iPhone sketch of the 1000 Islands Harbor Hotel
from the water, from author's photo

Built in the footprint of reclaimed land previously occupied by the Frink Snowplow factory, the Riverside (Cassidy) Hotel and the coal and passenger yard by the river, the hotel has become a popular wedding and conference venue for Clayton, as well as a great place to stay. From the river it sits behind the accompanying Clayton Harbor Municipal Marina, added since the hotel was built, and a popular place for overnighting with your boat.

If you are lucky when out there, you may see some interesting ships, from all over the world. Passenger liners small enough to fit in a Seaway Lock have become more numerous these days, plying the St. Lawrence and the Great Lakes. Tall ships, like the one pictured below the sketch of the liner Viking Octantis, are also occasional visitors. The Viking Octantis is not pictured on the river in the sketch, but was captured by

Brad Wood between lakes. She had already transited the St. Lawrence Sea Way. I believe the tall ship in the sketch below is the Lynx, but is unnamed because I wasn't sure which one she was when I sketched it from Dan Blank's photo. She is a two masted schooner, and there are several like her that appear on the river occasionally.

Ink sketch of the 1000 Islands Harbor Inn from Frink Park

(FROM PHOTO BY BRAD WOOD)

Passenger Liner Viking Octantis, from photo by Brad Wood, with permission

Tall Ship underway downbound, from photo by Dan Blank, with permission

I love drawing and sketching sailing ships, but I don't pretend that their rigging is exact or close to accurately but you can still tell they are sailing ships.

You will also see red and green numbered buoys marking the seaway channel. In winter, many are removed and sit in a colorful line on shore, many at Frink Park. You can't truly appreciate the size of these things until you see one on the dock at Frink Park. Gulls are often seen roosting on them. Other, smaller buoys are put out by Save the River or other community organizations, or private parties may put them out near their moorings.

Bob Carlysle's dock. From photo by Bob Carlysle, with permission.
You want to just sit there, don't you?

One of my favorite photo examples of one of many private docks on the river is one by Bob Carlysle of his new dock, seen above. It just invites you to dream of sitting there with a beer or a glass of wine and contemplating the sunset.

Back to the no wake zones, and private docks. Private docks are just that. If you've rented a boat, or you're in your own boat, short of an emergency or an invite by the owner, you are not welcome to moor at a private dock. Nor are you welcome to speed past, close up to such docks, as that is not only impolite, but it can also cause damage to the dock or boats tied to it. Please, be careful and courteous.

Devil's Oven, composite sketch from various photos and posters

The above ink sketch is of Devil's Oven, a tiny island without a structure, but a fascinating history. Or is it history? From my earliest memory of my tour guide brothers comes the heroic tale of Bill Johnson, a privateer (some would say pirate) during the War of 1812. We "won" by treaty because the British were occupied with other matters in Europe, and could not afford to bother with us. As a privateer, he attacked, captured, possibly pillaged, then burned a steam passenger ship moored off Wellesley Island. Allegedly, Johnson stole a chest full of British gold from the steamer Sir Robert Peel and hid out until the coast was clear in a cave, the dark entrance of which can be seen at the waterline in the sketch. Allegedly his daughter brought him food and drink, allowing him to survive his self-imposed exile. The real story is considerably less exiting, and is available on line, so I won't go into it here. Recently a large chunk of the stone that makes up the island fell off into the river, changing the look of Devil's Oven, and proving once more that nature is not immutable. She is always changing the face of the land.

As I've said several times, it's a big river. If you know where you're going, know there is open water ahead, speed isn't a problem. It's one reason there are so many "speedboats" still around. The wealthy used to have such boats custom built for them, and paid people to maintain and race them. That is the ancestry to the modern go-fast boats, like the ones present at poker run type events through the summer months. It's also the ancestry of the modern speedboat built for casual use, not racing. The Boldts, the Pullmans, the Emorys and other rich folk also built big boathouses and docks to accommodate them, as well as the large castle like homes scattered around the islands. Below is an antique "speedboat" running upriver in front of Twin Islands on a sunny day. The sketch is from a photo Erin Green took a few years ago, used with her permission.

Again, what is the happiest day in the life of a boat owner? The day they bought a boat. Now you know what their second happiest day is. The day they sold it. That's an old joke, but there is some truth to it. Boat ownership, particularly antique wooden boat ownership, is expensive. I've never owned a boat unless you count a couple of canoes, so how do I know that? Because I worked for a company in Clayton, Antique Boat America, ABA for short, for three summers, selling boats.

Twin Islands
FROM PHOTO BY ERIN GREENE
10/28/20

The above sketch was made from a photo by Erin Green. Twin Islands with a foot bridge between, and a runabout speeding by.

Shortly after I had five heart attacks and a quad bypass (CABG) to repair my heart, I applied for a job with ABA. I interviewed with Peter Mellon, the owner. Peter took pity on me, I think, and hired me. I worked with him, Doug Wild and Warren Metzger that first summer, learning as much about antique wooden boats as I could absorb while showing them, moving them around the showroom, and trying to sell them to potential buyers. The physical work involved got me back in shape from an arduous surgery and helped immensely in my mental recovery from that trauma as well. Peter was an expert in appraising antique boats, pleasing buyers, and an encyclopedia of information about them. Warren and Doug were also far more knowledgeable than I, but by the end of the next two summers I could keep up. Sadly, in the decades since, I have lost most of the information I worked hard to acquire. That has not dampened my love for boats, nor my almost childish delight in boat rides. You could say I got to associate with one of my favorite things without spending a dime on ownership. RIP, Peter, and Warren. I often recall your enthusiasm, your contribution to the community, and good humor.

SOME ISLANDS: THE ONES I KNOW BEST

One must have a boat or access to a boat to visit most Islands, and once there, most of them do not have roads. The largest islands, in order of size, are Wolfe (Can), Howe (Can), Wellesley (U.S.), Grindstone (U.S.), Hill, Grenadier (Can), and Carlton (U.S.). Only Wolf, Wellesley, Hill, and Howe have what we would consider "improved roads." The only one accessible by car is Wellesley. The others are only accessed by boat, with Howe and Wolfe having "regular 'car ferry service. Grindstone's cars were driven across the ice or brought by barge. Many have been abandoned there.

Of all the above islands, I have only set foot on a few. Those are Wolfe, Wellesley, Hill, and Grindstone. I've been on Cherry Island, Calumet Island, and Heart (Hart) Island as well for brief periods. I have driven on Wolfe and Wellesley, and actually spent quite a bit of time on the latter. This chapter includes a few sketches and some detail on what they are like.

The first is Grindstone, where, as mentioned earlier, I have only spent a few hours picnicking and visiting the convenient restrooms at Picnic Point, I have spent considerable time fishing right next to, or driving around Grindstone in a boat, however. As a young boy I got to spend a little time at Potter's Beach, a very popular spot now, but not so much back then. Next would be Cherry Island, where Carol and I were lucky enough to get a tour of Casa Blanca and the end of the island she sits on. I have already included a bit about Casa Blanca, but I will repeat the grayscale print iPad sketch I did (in color) of the Gargoyles on the grounds up-river from the house. The house and grounds are often home to catered weddings and other gatherings, including a charity tea hosted every year by the owner. I only wish I had got to know the story behind the gargoyles!

The front porch of Casa Blanca looks directly out on the river, with a view toward Alexandria Bay and the Seaway Channel. Our tour approached from upriver, and passed Twin Pines, the equally lovely large home at the head end of the Island. The channel between this series of islands from Cherry to Comfort Island is referred to as "Millionaire's Row," because at the turn of 19th century a group of wealthy people purchased the islands and built estates on them. Most of them are large Victorians, like Casa Blanca. The group includes Devil's Oven, which does not have a structure on It. Again, I have spent lots of time around these islands in a boat, but except for Cherry Island, never set foot on them.

I have very few pictures of Wolfe Island and have not yet done a sketch from any of the ones I do have, But we have driven the length of the island a couple of times, all the way to the light house and what used to be a Canadian Customs house at the foot. My father used to stop there and check in with Customs when we fished off Wolfe Is-land, each year he renewed our Canadian fishing licenses. I don't know if it's still used. The island is home to the village of Marysville, which is the terminus for the car ferry from Kingston to Wolfe Island.

The terminus for the car ferry from Wolfe to Cape Vincent is at the end of the road across the island from Marysville.

Casa Blanca
Ink sketch From the author's photo

Twin Pine on Cherry Island, ink sketch from author's photo

Carol and I had lunch at a nice little restaurant on Brown's

Bay, just Northeast of town. You can see Kingston from the beach there, and there is a small motel. We've always meant to stay there, but it never happened. Since the pandemic the Cape Vincent ferry service, run by George Horne, has been less dependable due to labor shortage, I'm told. It's normally well run and is a great trip. When you drive from Clayton on Route 12 E on the way to "The Cape" you can see Carlton and Wolfe Islands when there is a break in the trees along 12, and almost all the way to the Tibbetts Point lighthouse. You can also see the many windmills scattered on that end of the island. Their location makes great sense, as there is nearly a constant wind off Lake Ontario. Often a very strong wind. The early settlers of Wolfe and Carleton Islands must have been a hardy lot!

We've never been to Howe Island, but I have known folks from there. Like Wolfe, there is a community, a ferry, and roads. We have often said we would go there one day, but we never have.

Wellesley Island and Hill Island are very familiar ground to us. We've camped there, visited friends there, and nearly annually, driven from head to foot, and side to side. Wellesley 1000 Island State Park has a great campground, a beach and a marina. It looks right out at Canada; so close in fact that people have been known to swim across. The rough sketch through the trees of the Canadian shore from my brother's family's favorite campsite shows just how close.

You might see an eagle, like the sketch I did for a watercolor from a photo by Andrew Kane taken on Wellesley Island. You can also visit Minna Anthony Common Nature Center, where exhibits and programs describe the flora and fauna and history of the Island.

Canada through trees on the shore of Wellesley
Island State Park from author's photo

Grayscale print of watercolor of an Eagle on
Wellesley Island, right after a meal -
From photo by Andrew Kane, with permission

Minna Anthony Common Nature Center, ink sketch from photo by Joseph Leskoske, with permissionRoute 100 on Wellesley Island, through the golf course to the right

The photo following the nature center sketch is a grayscale print of a painting I did from my photo of County Route 100 as it passes the golf course at the Northeast end of Wellesley Island. This course and the Country Club it is part of are in the footprint of the Boldt Estate. Route 100 runs from the head of the Island to its foot. In my opinion it is one of the prettiest drives in Upstate New York.

At the head end of Wellesley is a settlement founded originally as a religious retreat. Thousand Islands Park is one of the most unique places in the islands. Victorian mostly summer dwellings line the geometrically laid out streets of the community, all well-kept and decorated. I have some photos from last year but have yet to sketch them. I do have a few sketches, which I hope will illustrate the uniqueness of this community.

Jefferson County Rte 100 on Wellesley Island, grayscale
print of watercolor from photo by author

Rock Island Light from Thousand Islands Park
near pavilion, from author's photo

Grayscale print of Thousand Islands Park Pavilion,
colored pencil sketch from author's photo

(Above) One of the author's favorite homes in Thousand Islands Park,
sketched from author's 2003 photo (below) 1000 Islands Park Paviliaon from
Debbie McDonald Photo

The next photo is of an island with three names. Hub Island, Just Room Enough Island, and Mother-in-Law Island. Last I heard it is for sale or was just sold. This photo of it was taken from the shuttle to and from Boldt Castle. I'm not sure of the origin of the Hub Island name, but the other two are obvious. It has the look of a place one might exile one's troublesome or meddlesome mother-in-law, and there is just room enough on it for a cottage. It does flood, occasionally, but at present water levels it is high and dry.

Just Room Enough Island, grayscale print of watercolor
painting from author's photo

The island is located in the town of Alexandria Bay, and not a
long boat ride from Wellesley or the village of Alexandria Bay.

Moonrise over Hill Island, preliminary sketch for watercolor by author
from photo by Karen Millspaugh, with permission

Hill Island is separated from Wellesley Island by a narrow passage from the Lake of the Isles. The "lake" is really a blind bay between Islands. The islands are joined by two stone and concrete arch bridges, and the U.S.-Canada border separates them.Once you drive from the U.S. on that bridge over the channel, you are in Canada. The area between the bridges and the Canadian Customs station is tax neutral and contains a duty-free store on each side of the road and an observation tower, which can be seen in the sketch, backed by a full Hunter's Moon. Karen Milspaugh's photo would have been taken from a boat in Canadian waters. This is one of my favorite watercolors, with fall foliage and a dark sky.

The next island featured is my favorite, though I don't get to visit it that often. My high school art teacher, James (Prof)

DeStefano often painted Rock Island Light and gave my dad one of his paintings. Sadly, it has been lost over the decades and many moves we have undertaken since, and we no longer have it. It has been one of the most drawn or painted subject in my collection, with at least six examples. I also have many photos of it. Here are two of the art works.

Simple sketch of Rock Island light from a crop of author's photo

Rock Island Light and full moon, sketch for watercolor from
photo by Debbie McDonald, with permission.

I wish I could include color photos, as the second, based on
a photo by Debbie Mc Dowell, is one of my favorite angles
to have captured in both watercolor and a digitally painting.
A painting needs a subject, and I have been lucky enough to
be able to use so many photographers 'beautifully composed
photos of the subjects I love most - 1000 Islands scenes. I also
use my own shots, but I can't be there as often or as long as I'd
like, and I am running out of material from which to paint or
sketch.

You can find many of these great photographers and their work on Facebook, on the 1000 Islands River Rats Now and Then, St. Lawrence Seaway Ship Watchers, Thousand Islands River Views, and other river fan sites. Some have their own professional sites as well. If you are an artist, and you ask politely, many will give permission to paint the subject of a photo. Please, be sure to ask first. If someone says no, you cannot use their work. If you do use their work, with permission, you must include a citation. Artists, professional or not, deserve and are legally entitled to credit for their work.

Just upriver from Rock Island is a group of three islands: Round Island, Little Round Island and North Colborne Island. The latter has two little islets trailing down river after it, a 90-degree mirror of the three Islands in close approximation of their order in size – something not obvious from the water, but clear from the chart below. Round Island was mostly owned by Charles Emery, with investors, who built a previously mentioned resort hotel, the Frontenac, in the middle of the largest island.

Little Round Island was not permitted to have any structures on it at the time I was growing up in Clayton, but at some point since I left, development was allowed, as there are now summer homes there. North Colborne has, as far as I know, no structures. My dad and I used to drift fish from the head end of Round Island, past Little Round Island to the foot of the big island. Tour boats used to frequent that channel (later they were not allowed to) and a tour boat at speed throws a considerable wake. We would have to start the engine and be sure to keep the bow pointed at that wake, quartering it, to avoid a roll. I assume that was hard on the docks on round Island.

Round Island Post Office, grayscale print of digital painting on iPad

I have lost count of the number of times I have transited that channel then, or since. The last was when Bernie Miller took me out for a boat ride to Alex Bay and back and let me pilot his boat. It was either then or another ride with Chris Muggleton in his boat that I took the photo that was the reference for the above iPencil/iPad painting I did. I made two – one of the Post Office with Summer colors, one with Fall colors approximated in. This post office is still in service today. I think you can stop there and mail a letter which will be postmarked Round Island, NY.

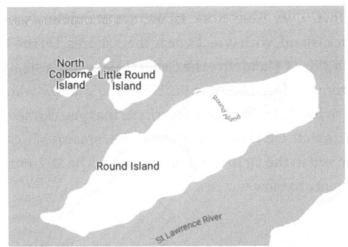
Map of Round Island group

Returning to Clayton you pass Chapman Shoal light, a spot where many a ship has found its bottom, some sinking nearby, some limping in to dock. In the area between Rock Island and Chapman Shoal is a literal ship graveyard. In fact wreck diving in the entire length of the narrow channel between Alex Bay and Clayton is popular, as the area is full of sunken hulls that divers love to explore.

Rough sketch of the relative position of Round and Little Round Islands viewed from Frink Park

Just down river from Rock Island are Mandolin Island and Frederick Island, with wrecks near their shores. On the Fishers Landing side of Mandolin, the General Hancock, a steel hulled ferry from the late 1800's, is visible in the shallow water. The river is so low at the date this is written that you can see nearly the entire Hull. Off Frederick Island is the remains of a car ferry that burned in the 1930's. If you are a diver, the St. Lawrence is a great place to view wrecks.

On the shore to your left past Chapman Shoal is Washington Island. When I was a boy, it was pasture land, with an oil pipeline leading from a spot where tankers could moor to pump fuel oil and heating oil ashore. I don't remember a time when cows were pastured there, but they were early in the 20th century. There were few trees, mostly brush and grass. In the 1970's Gerald and Leo Ingerson and investors built a causeway and bridge across the shallow water between Washington Island and the Northeast shore at Gardener Street in Clayton. The Island was then developed for luxury homes, and a community was built out there. You can drive out and ride around, but it is all private property, so best not to linger unless invited. It is now a beautifully landscaped park-like development, and a great addition to the Village of Clayton.

Whether you are out on the river or sitting in Frink Park, there are myriad things to see. These are just a few of the sights for you to marvel at. I've never seen anyone ignore them. Almost everything is something you don't see at home. Unless, of course, you live here by the river.

Notebook sketch of the view toward the river from the
beginning of the causeway from author's photo.

View toward the island from the Causeway near the
mainland shore, from author's photo

FROM THE WASHINGTON ISLAND CAUSWAY

Another Causeway view, from author's photo

Cargo carrier upbound in front of Calumet Island, from author's photo.

Gas tanker upbound in front of Boldt Castle, from author's photo.

Frink Park pavillion from Riverside Drive, from author's photo

OTHER MEMORIES

My first real connected memories are of a house on Jane Street in Clayton that no longer exists. I have a photo somewhere, which accompanied one of my Thousand Islands Sun articles. It's of me, about age 3 or 4, in an old metal car with pedal power. My first memories of my grandmother were from that house. She used to read to me from a book called Freddy the Fireman, possibly because we lived right downhill from the Clayton Fire Department fire siren, of which I was mightily frightened at about age 3 when it went off for VE and VJ Day. When I got older, I thought for a while I might want to be a fireman when I grew up. I never got there.

We moved from that house to 725 Beecher Street. Below is an ink drawing of the Beecher house as it looked in winter, in approximately 1946, which I did for the current owner. It really has not changed all that much. As a sickly child I spend a lot of time lying in bed, in a small room on the first floor. My brothers Jack and Jim went off to serve in the Air Force, and I moved into the back bedroom upstairs with my brother, Dick. My mom and dad occupied the front bedroom, and the third bedroom was my mother's sewing room, and guest room. When my grandma came to visit, she stayed in the room I vacated downstairs.

My most vivid memories of that house are pleasant. My dad sometimes brought home a record player he borrowed from the school. It played 33 and 45 RPM records, and one of the records played often was Christmas greetings from England, where they were both stationed at two different Air Bases, as Air Patrolmen -AP's. My mom and dad recorded "In the Money (Ain't We Got Fun)" on one of the school machines, and I seem to remember they sent copies to Jack and Jim. Mom had a beautiful singing voice, and my dad was a bass.

We enjoyed Thanksgiving dinners in the dining room right off the front door, and always had a Christmas tree in the front parlor, which faced the street. Until I was old enough to go by myself, my brothers took me sledding behind the school, on a big hill that now looks very small to me, as an adult.

I inherited my oldest brother Jack's red 26" bicycle, which I had learned to ride to great ridicule from my brothers, graduating from a smaller bike with training wheels. The freedom of finally learning to ride a bike was exhilarating.Bryce Baker and I used to ride everywhere, Including up and down McCarn's Hill on route 12. It seemed much bigger then. I suspect the exercise improved my asthmatic lungs a good deal, as I outgrew the asthma attacks when I reached puberty. Unfortunately, in the same period I acquired a taste for unfiltered cigarettes, because my friends smoked, and it was not cool if you didn't. Twenty-six years later I quit, wishing I had never started. Asthmatics should never smoke.

725 Beecher Street, ca 1946. Ink sketch from a 1946 family photo

I've covered our move to Graves Street in an earlier chapter, but the memories there are good ones as well. My brothers returned from their service in the Air Force, and went off to college, Jim to St. Lawrence and Jack to Syracuse. Dick graduated from high school and went on to join Jim at St. Lawrence. When I left Clayton and went to Syracuse in 1960, they had all graduated. Jack and Dick went on to graduate programs at S.U. my sophomore and junior years, by which time my mom, dad, and I had left Clayton for Syracuse.

I learned to drive on Graves Street hill in Dick's old Plymouth stick shift "three on the tree". I remember calling my first real "date" from the upstairs phone, so Mom and Dad would not hear. I had to drive to Watertown to pick her up. We went to a movie, and she agreed to be my Senior Prom date. She was a career model, a real beauty. I never saw her again, but coincidentally, it was my other best friend, Jim Marshall., was the one who "fixed me up" with her, as a blind date. Six years later he and his future first wife Gladys "fixed me up," with another blind date, my wife of 57 years, Carol, who was as beautiful as Jim's cousin, my first "date."

Our reason for coming to Clayton from Mooers, NY was this school, pictured above. It was constructed at the end of the third decade of the 20th Century. Dad had been principal of the Mooers Central School, and this was a step up for him, as the Clayton District was just centralizing at the time. He was, by all accounts including mine, a fair man, a strong disciplinarian, and a good principal. Referring to the photo, his office was behind the center two windows of the far-left wing of the school, with the main office the next two windows to the right. Left of my dad's office was the board room, where the school board met. As yearbook photographer, I may have taken this photo in 1959 or 1969.

The house at the top of Graves Street Hill. From author's photo

CLAYTON CENTRAL SCHOOL ca 1960

My dad's school. He was principal here from 1944 to
1961. Ink sketch from CCS yearbook photo

You can see the large glass block windows of the gym/
auditorium peeking out at the far left, behind the pine tree.
The bushes under the office windows were a great place for
a little kid to hide, knowing his father was just behind the
wall at his back. Above the office, to the far left, was the high
school World and American History teacher Mr. Katsmayer's
room, adjoining the school library overseen by Miss Kelley, the
librarian. The large windows above the central door let great
quantities of sunlight into the library. It was one of my favorite
places to spend time. To the right of the library and below, on
the first floor, was the classroom wing, with primary grades K
-4. Upstairs, the grade 7-12 homerooms, biology, health, and
driver training rooms were directly above K-4. A third wing led
back away from that central door to the auditorium backstage
doors, the music rooms, janitor's room, kitchen and cafeteria
on the first floor. The art room, business ed, home economics,
Latin, and physics/chemistry/photography lab were directly
above on the second floor. The latter also served as the Math

teacher's headquarters and 10th grade homeroom.

In the early to mid 50's a new wing was added at the east end of the building, containing a basketball court sized gym, and new 5th and 6th grade rooms.

In the latter is where I spent my 12th and 13th years of age in school. There was no graduation into "Junior High" from those rooms, other than the mere fact that we moved upstairs to another wing. For the first time we experienced moving from room to room as well. Before that all instruction took place in one room. Also included above the gym in the new addition was a large room that could be divided down the middle, with a door on each side of the divider that could make two rooms out of one. I don't recall it often being used that way. Most of the time it was used as a 9th grade home room and a huge study hall.

The impressive main entrance was rarely used, and then mostly for school photos. You could display an entire class there, using the steps as risers so no one got left out, no matter how short. Almost everyone entered or left by the door that can't be seen in the photo, next to the gym, directly past my dad's office. I always wondered if he had a hand in that strategy.

I've mentioned the Beecher and Graves Street houses we lived in for most of our time in Clayton. What might not be obvious if you've never been to Clayton is their proximity to the school. Dad's office was a mere hundred yards or so away from the front door of the Beecher St. house, 500 to 600 feet from the Graves St. house. The same could be said of his children's commute to and from school. Dick and I had but to walk those 500 feet or so past the bus garage and into the entrance by the Music Rooms; me to 5th grade, Dick to one of the upstairs 9th grade homerooms. No walking a mile uphill each way through deep snow tales for us. Also there was the fact that school would be closed on days like that: no bus traffic was possible.

Living so close had lots of benefits, but one quirk on the downside was the proximity to my dog. I got my first dog, a Collie we named Mike, when I turned 13. We all loved Mike, and like all dogs he returned that love and then some. While that might not seem like a problem to most, it created one for our dad. When the door at home opened, he often escaped, and where did he go? He followed his master, me, to school. Since my scent disappeared after he reached the nearest door, he waited until someone came out, then went right in. Sometimes he would go to the office end of the long corridor to the right, sometimes he would go right to my 6th grade classroom, and whine outside the door. He was a big dog, and some people were afraid of him, though he would never have hurt anyone. The 6th grade classroom phone would ring, with my dad or someone at the office at the other end. "Tell Joel to get his dog and take it home," would be the message. Miss Fitzgerald would send me to go get Mike, and he would dutifully follow me home, where I would clip his collar to the lead fastened to a trolly on a wire from the back door to a pole about 40 feet away.

There he would sit, mournfully watching me head back to school. We did that until near the end of my Senior year in high school when it became obvious that we could not keep him when I went away to college.

We knew he would become a burden on my mother, one which she was not willing to assume. We "re-homed" Mike with a family that lived on a farm outside town. I never saw him again. Around the end of my senior year, Dad got Mom a miniature grey poodle. His pedigree name was Button, short for Petit Argent Buton, or Little Silver Button. She had Button until around 1973, a fewyears after my dad passed away. He had named his boat "Buton," after Mom's dog. He would never admit it, but he loved that dog as much as she did. Mom never had another dog.

Our house was surrounded by large trees. Most are gone but have been replaced by trees grown almost as big as the originals. A huge silver maple stood at the right front corner of the enclosed porch as you faced the house, overhanging the porch roof and the driveway. It survived the ice storms in 1952 and 1959 but has since been replaced. Silver Maples are not long-lived.

It was a great climbing tree. Bryce and I used to climb up to its third tier of branches and pretend we were invisible, that the tree was a fort, etc. What young boys do. I eventually outgrew tree climbing except from necessity, but that did not stop my cat, Rusty, from climbing up there and – well who know what he thought when he was up there. One spring day one of Dick's friends, one of the Carpenter boys, came to see Dick. I was out working on my bike in the yard, and he showed up with his Beagle. He and Dick stood talking for a bit, and suddenly we heard the dog barking, and a yowl. Looking up in the tree we saw Rusty, poised to jump, with his back arched, hissing down at the dog. Suddenly he launched himself, 12 pounds of yellow tiger cat with long needle-sharp claws, down at the dog's back.

Now I had seen this cat come home one day dragging a full-grown buck rabbit, still alive and kicking, across the back field, meowing the whole time. He was one tough cat. He fastened his claws to that dog's hide, facing the dog's tail, and held on. The dog took off kiyi-ing up the dirt section of Graves St. at least a hundred feet before Rusty tired of the game and jumped off. That dog would never get near our place again. Couldn't say I blamed him.

There were lots of things about that house, just thinking about it, that come to mind. Some other time I may write about them, but I have other things to add here. The next sketch was done from my photo taken a decade or so ago. Carol and I were in Watertown for lunch, and when we go there, we usually have something she or I or both want to do.

This day we ate pizza on Public Square and wandered around the west end of the square so I could do a memory trip, and maybe shoot a few pictures. Being the loquacious old man I am, I had to recite some stories from my past visits to Watertown. She politely pretends to listen when I do that.

The Arcade, Watertown, NY

In this case we were outside the entrance to the arcade, and I was telling her about the Woolworth's that used to be there, and how my mother used to bring me to Watertown a lot to have my very heavy eyeglasses adjusted or repaired. Woolworths had a lunch counter, and we occasionally ate there. Loved their ice cream and milkshakes. My optician was in the space just to the left of the Arcade entrance. That storefront has been many things since then, but at the time it was an optician's store. It later moved across the hall to the right in the photo above, but the last time we were in there not long ago it was an optician's office again.

On the day this shot was taken they had set up tables and chairs for a wedding or party. When I was a little kid, and a teen, the brick floor, the glass skylighted ceiling and balcony rails along the open second floor always caught my eye. I've seen a few arcades like this since, but this is the one that comes to mind when I hear or see the word. There was a news stand at the other end, off on the right by the door to the alley between Arsenal and Stone, where I used to buy comics, and Popular Mechanics. I recall the smell of Karmel Korn with the image, as there was a store right nearby the optician, and Mom always had to pop in there to buy some, which we could smell every one of the 18 or so miles home. Kind of like a takeout pizza run.

At one time there was also a Fanny Farmer confectioner's shop up front facing the square, and Mom loved their chocolates. To this day I find that sights, sounds and smells can bring back some good memories. They tend to gloss over the fact that, without my very heavy, thick glasses I was almost legally blind. Now that I have had cataract surgery, I have nearly forgotten how that feels. I've worn glasses, thick ones, for most of my life, ever since the age of 2. Hearing people say "hey, four eyes," lost the hurt a long time ago. But when I go to Watertown, I think of the many trips I made there with my Mom.

Another building in which I spent lots of time, and the sight of which invokes fond memories, is the Hawn Memorial Library. I have frequented libraries since around the age of 4, accompanied early on in life by my mom or grandmother. Mom used to love Ngaio Marsh's mysteries, and always asked the librarian about her newest book, and other mystery writers of the day. I would sit with a Freddy the fireman or Tuggy the Tugboat book and try to read it. Somewhere between 4 and 5, I could.

Last year I took a folder of my watercolors with me to Clayton in case I got the chance to show them. I usually kept them in the car, just in case. One day we parked

Hawn Memorial Library. Grayscale print of Digital Painting from author's photograph

right in this spot, in front of the library, planning to walk around, and to stop in the River Muse art gallery across the street. When we returned, after an unsuccessful stop at the gallery, I did something I often do with things I am carrying. I put the folder on top of the car; and drove away with it still there. When I got home, I looked for the folder in the back seat, where I was sure I had placed it. It wasn't there. I had a flash of memory, of putting it on the roof, and was suddenly painfully aware of what had happened. Hundreds of hours of work had been lost, potentially scattered along John Street on the way home. I got right back in the car and drove back to the same parking spot. I went into the gallery, then the library, and told someone in both places what had apparently happened. Embarrassed, I left my name, aware that it was not likely they had survived or anyone would return them. On the way home I drove slowly along the route we had previously taken, but no folder.

That afternoon someone from the library called, saying that a patron had found my folder and turned it in. I never found out who, but I want to thank them. The originals of many of the prints in this book were in that folder. I have digital copies of all my paintings, but this would have been a blow. Again, thank you!

The print below is of the C Way Resort Motel just outside Clayton on Route 12. It is from a watercolor I did using a photo I took when we stayed there in 1990 for the 30th Clayton Central School Class of 1960 reunion. The school we attended, the one in the earlier sketch, is no longer the only school in the district. That building is now the Guardino Elementary School. But many classes continue to have their own reunion, long after CCS was no longer home to K-12. This particular year we had our reunion at a very familiar place, one which Carol and I, and everyone else who enters town from the south on Route 12 frequently pass, and in our case, look forward to seeing, as it marks the end of a long trip. We remember staying there for the 1970 reunion, for example, when my mother accompanied us to Clayton, and baby sat for our then two-year old son Kevin.

The C Way Resort Motel and Pool, grayscale print from watercolor based on author's 1990 photo

Our 1990 reunion was held at McCormic's Restaurant, and I had been asked to be the MC for the dinner that evening. During dinner I got a phone call from my mother, who informed me that Kevin had locked himself in the bathroom, and what should she do? I asked her if she had a bobby pin and told her how to unlock the door from the outside using it. She was very excited, and a little upset that I would do that, instead of coming back to the motel to do it for her. She eventually forgave me, but we've had a laugh at that memory occasionally when driving past the motel. It is still a popular spot, with Natali's Restaurant right across the road. You can't miss it.

The next sketch is of James Street back in the 60's when Kennedy Drugs was in the building that had been Pulver's and is now Michael Ringer's Gallery. I don't recall the exact year Kinney Drugs came to town, and Kennedy's was no longer there, but I can recall shopping at Kennedy's before that. I took the photo this sketch was based on in the winter of 1959 for the 1960 Calumet yearbook. Winters were harsh in Clayton back then, and still are, though it seems to be changing. It's a very rough sketch, but there is snow on the ground. You can see the sign for Walroth's Bar and Grille, which is now the Lost Navigator. Sketchily drawn across the street you can see Cantwell's Creamery, now The Koffee Kove Restaurant. I sometimes have to remind observers that a sketch is a sketch and, depending on the amount of time spent on it, may be quite as "sketchy" as this one. I include it, rather than the photo, as this book is about my art. And sometimes, a sketch is all I need. This one evokes all the memories it needs to, and I could nearly do it from memory.

Things change, in Clayton and the rest of the world. I've mentioned that I've heard and read the Clayton waterfront described as "picturesque," and "quaint" It is, and it really has not changed much since Charles Emory's wife allegedly called it something else.

Kennedy Pharmacy and James Street, from author's 1959 photo

Clayton waterfront, and the wave attenuator as seen
from the old pier. From author's photo

One change after I left for a higher education was the addition
of an L shaped pier and a floating wave attenuator to reduce
the effect of wave action on the waterfront and the pier.
High water and wind a couple of years ago damaged the new
Riverwalk along the shore here, and grant funds have been
used to repair and replace these things. I've seen photos and
video of the waves crashing ashore, and it's evident that little
could have been done to prevent this. Water and wind are a
powerful combination of energy forces, and we can but hope
this doesn't turn into a regular event. Thomas a Kempis said,
"Man proposes, but God disposes." One cannot argue with that.
The evidence is everywhere. If you are a non-believer, change
that to Nature and it still works.

Town of Orleans park in Fisher's landing, sketch from author's photo

This next is from Summer of 2022. A beauty of a sunset at Rotary Park, boats bobbing gently the docks. Originally an ink sketch, I also turned it into a digital painting and a watercolor painting. One day we will get to have dinner and desert at DePrinzio's. You can see their patio in the center.

Dance Hall, bowling alley, Marina, empty lot. A sketch
from my photo of the location of all three

View across 1000 Islands Harbor Inn resort lawn and Frink park toward lighted Calumet water tower. iPad painting from author's photo.

I can't think of a better way to round out the artistic, memories in paint, ink and pixels than this view. I neve tire of it, or the one from the benches at Frink Park. As a last piece, I give you an ink sketch/illustration from a photo by Maryanne Chadwick, with her permission. To all who Facebook post - a wine glass in the hand, on a rail, a dock post in front of a beach fire,or a rock with the river in the back ground, or just enjoying the feel of the breeze, Salud. May your days on vacation or living by the river be happy, healthy and filled with love.

Joel

BENCH BUDDIES

"Regulars" at the river, whether regular summer folk like us or full-time residents, meet and get to know other regulars. If you're just visiting, you should talk to people. You may not become long term friends, but you will find out something interesting. People from all over, hear about, and learn about the St. Lawrence River and the 1000 Islands, Clayton or Alex Bay or Cape Vincent in particular. This book has been mostly about Clayton, and certainly books have been written about the other two towns that have a unique position on the river. When people hear about the 1000 Islands, they are often drawn to them, and not surprisingly, many become "regulars", or even permanent residents, summer or year round. They have found something in each town that draws them. Some, like us, grew up here, vacationed with their family here as children, or lived here for a short time with family or a relative, then moved away and came back.. People who visit for the first time often come back and become "regulars." Our friends the Millers are from Canada. Bernie has many relatives in the U.S. They've been coming back for decades, nearly every summer. Clayton draws people.

When we first began to summer in Clayton, in the early 2000's, we met many people, some new, some old friends. But a particular group became new friends, with whom we have been fortunate enough to have developed a lasting relationship. Over the years, even after we stopped spending full summers in Clayton, we have looked forward to coming back, renewing our "Bench Buddy" friendships, and perhaps acquiring new ones. It has been an amorphous group in the last twenty years. People age and are no longer able to travel, or pass into that great beyond, where they may find a new river to love. People move away, and the "commute" becomes too long. But there is a core of folks who know each other, and look forward to meeting "next summer," at the river. We don't always get a photo of them, so I am missing many, but I have included some recent and some old photos as a tribute to the ones who we see every year, and those who can't come back, or who are no longer with us. If I have missed you, it is my memory lapse, and I can but offer my apologies. I will end this tale with the photos I have. No sketches, as my people drawing skills have yet to surface, and may never. This chapter is more about friends and Clayton memories than my art,. Because the exact origins of the group, or whose idea it was to congregate at the river to watch the sunset is lost in my memories somewhere, I'll begin with some names and photos of the "original" group.

At first it was rare to find any but our neighbors at French Creek Marina and their friends at the "Bench O 'Knowledge," as George called us when we first gathered on the old wood benches at Rotary Park. As a result, there are few photos of them, even fewer of any of us sitting together at the park. I have included photos taken at French Creek Marina parties where some of us also gathered, so that I may include them.

A little bit about our history of our getting into the Bench Buddy group. In 2003, Carol and I decided to buy a Jayco RV trailer. We had been looking at RVs, both trailers and self-contained, for at least a decade, dreaming of the open road and all the places we could go if we bought one. A banker friend told me, "Don't do it. The things depreciate faster than a car, and you'd be better off renting," so we did not buy one before retirement.

We did rent, and it was a nightmare. The four-year-old Winnebago we rented had an ants 'nest in the overhead cupboards, and we had to remove it the second day of our trip. The day after we found the nest, we were heading down out of the Blue Ridge Mountains at the northern end on very steep winding switchbacks. I was saving the brakes by engine braking and bent a push rod. The engine began clattering and I had use just the brakes the rest of the way down to Rte 81, then limp slowly back up the mountains from Route 81 to Charlottesville, VA. I've never been passed on a hill so often in 64 years of driving. It was 100 degrees the next day, and we couldn't run the AC. We stayed at a campground and took the Winnie to a GMC dealer, who gave us the bad news. I called my friend, from whom I had rented it and, though unhappy about it, he arranged to pay for the short block and valve replacement repair needed. Good side: after renting an air-conditioned car, we got to visit Monticello, and saw the first run of Star Wars in an air-conditioned theater the same day. Bad side: without the engine the Mini-Winnie had no AC. Right then we decided, there was no way would we own one.

But we kept looking at them, for fun, until one day in 2003 we found the perfect one. A 24 'Jayco travel trailer with a kitchen, dining area, bedroom and full (though small) bath, and no motor to maintain. We had not given it much thought until Fall of 2003. But by October, a great weather period in Tucson, AZ, we were the proud owners of a like new 1998 Jayco travel trailer. To tow it we bought a 1998 Dodge Ram 1500 pickup with full trailer package; whatever that means.

That summer of 2003, we had been in Clayton for an all-class reunion for Clayton Central School. While there we looked at French Creek Marina, because one of our classmates lived there in the summer, and it seemed better than renting an apartment. After a couple of short haul dry run trips, we decided to take it from Tucson to New York in May of 2004 and stay in Clayton for the summer. People have often, due to our many moves, called us gypsies. Now we could be.

In May of 2004 I drove the trailer to the Atlanta area, where our son Kevin was living. Carol was working until the following week, so I was alone. I stopped in Van Horn in West Texas, Dallas, and Jackson Mississippi. In that shakedown period, I unconsciously accepted that I was not going to take the trailer back to Arizona. The trailer and the 1998 Dodge 1500 Ram pickup made a 44-foot vehicle out of the two units. The length of many long-haul semis. "4 Wheelers" don't understand large vehicles 'problems. Just as I got to Atlanta a piece of plumbing under the trailer came loose, and rattled all the way to the campground. I got a handyman who knew trailers to fix it like new at relatively low cost, but it was a nerve wracking drive until the repair was done. Let's say it was not a pleasant trip at times, and that I'm not cut out to be a frequent long-haul trucker. When Carol got to Atlanta, I did not immediately tell her what I had in mind: leaving the trailer at the marina and using it as a New York base. Once there we discussed it, and decided to rent a "permanent" spot across the street. We were there for four years. It was four of the best years of our lives.

The first photo is from a neighborhood barbecue on the lawn between our trailer and the Pulver's motor home. Sandy Thompson, Harry Pulver and Marian Pulver are in the foreground. I can't recall the gentleman's name in the background adjusting our grill, but he was a neighbor also. Sandy and Al Thompson lived down the dirt street from us on the same side of the road. Our space was directly West of the River View Apartments, a senior housing community off Strawberry Lane.

Our Jayco trailer was in the Southeast corner of the RV park, 4 or 5 lots in from Strawberry Lane, diagonally across from the shower house/laundry room. On our North Side were Glen Helmer and Deloris Cole. Glen is the man next to Jim Kendall in the photo below.

I graduated from Clayton Central School with Jim. The Kendalls lived just down the street from us. These two shots were taken in the yard between us and the Pulver's 40' motorhome, and on the unroofed, unscreened deck I built that year. Our roll out awning was the roof. The next year we had Jim Schnauber's crew build an 8X24 'screen house on top of the deck I had built myself, the year before. In the first year we made friends with our neighbors, and some of us developed the habit of going down to the river, nearly every night, and sitting on the benches I so well recalled from my youth. Sometimes, when the benches were full of happy tourists, we went to the benches at Frink Park, but until Frink Park was remodeled, we more frequently sat on the benches along the pipe railing above Rotary Park. George and his wife, whose last name I have lost over 17 years lived in Clayton and often joined us, along with the group from French Creek Marina. Over the summer it became a habit. Finish dinner, sit on the porch for a bit, then walk down to the river and sit talking with friends while waiting for one of the beautiful St. Lawrence sunsets to manifest.

Harry Pulver, Carol Charles, Jim Kendall, Glenn Helmer

Left to right: Sandy Thompson, Harry Pulver, Marian Pulver

FRENCH CREEK MARINA, CLAYTON, NY 5/2005

Our summer home in Clayton from 2004 to 2010, with finished screen deck. The Pulvers were to the right, you can see Glen and Delores 'trailer to the left and behind ours. We shared a lawn with the Pulvers.

Dolores Cole, Carol Charles, Glenn Helmer

There were often lively group discussions about nearly everything. Sometimes politics, when the discussion grew hotter than usual, but more often about friends, boats, activities, places to go, etc.I don't recall the exact discussion, or the timing, but sometime that summer, George coined the phrase "Bench O 'Knowledge." George was a man of wit, and strong opinions. One day he just spoke up out of the blue and said something about our being the Bench O 'Knowledge. I'm pretty sure it was not meant either as an insult or a compliment, but the name, or the phrase, stuck. From that point on, we knew ourselves as the Bench Buddies of "The Bench O 'Knowledge."

Glen and Delores came back in 2005, but moved to a campground in Virginia in 2006, and were replaced by Mert and Daryl Johnson, who moved into their spot

Carol Charles, Mert and Daryl Johnson at Frink Park

next door in a motorhome. They joined the group on the benches and fit right in. In the background of the photo, taken before the new pavilion was built, is the Herald House/1000 Islands Inn. You can see the sign that this year, after the street renovation was finished, lies abandoned at the back of the building. The benches in the photo are at the top of a stepped area of wooden amphitheater seats you see in one of the earlier sketches of the original Frink Park. Said seats were not as comfortable as these benches.

The first photo below shows four more of our neighbors, Jean and George Brick, and Glenn and Iris Dickenson at a party in Dickenson's side yard. Their trailer was sited next to and above Wahl Drive, visible in the background looking West. Wahl Drive, of course, was named after the founder and owner, Wilbert Wahl, with whom my brother Jim graduated from Clayton Central School in 1951.

Jean and George Brick, Glenn and Iris Dickenson

The photo below is of two of my high school friends, Sara (DeStefano) Norton and Carolyn (Skeet) Vincent/Bourgeois, with Carol and Ron Houppert in the background. They often visited with us in Clayton over the last two decades. The other person in the photo is a friend of Skeet's, Tracy Longway. Visible at back left is Reinman's Hardware, and on the right, over Skeet's shoulder, is the Empty space left where the Golden Anchor used to be, and the new building with Freighters and DiPrinzio's Kitchen, and apartments above now fills. This spot at Rotary Park is where the "Bench O'Knowledge" was conceived. That corner of the seating area was usually empty when we got there around 7pm, so it became our default seating area when we were not at Frink Park. When the new pavilion was built, we could now sit out of a misty rain, on dry seats. Which was and is where you would find us most nights.

Sara (DeStefano) Norton and Carolyn (Skeet) Vincent/Bourgeois,
with Carol and Ron Houppert in the background.

In 2014 Carol and I rented the Muggleton's Boat House on Riverside Drive. One night during our two weeks there that rather cool summer the Bench Buddies congregated at "our" place, where there is a 180-degree view of the river and the 1000 Islands Boat Museum across the bay. That is where the next shot was taken, on the glass enclosed porch/dining room of the Boat House.

Front Row: Carol Charles, Grace DeBoer, Sandy Thompson.
Back Row: Sid (Bud) DeBoer, Al Thompson, Joel Charles

I'm the only one not smiling because I had just tripped the iPhone camera's timer and run around the table to be in the shot. Hence the extra dumb look on my face.

The next two photos show us in our favorite environment. There is even WiFi, albeit spotty, and lots of seating. Of course, as in the first photo, the river weather is unpredictable, and as is evident in the photo, a bit coolish, with a stiff breeze at times. The pavilion is open, so there is little protection except from a West wind. But rarely is the area cold enough or wet enough in July to keep people who are devoted to sunsets away from the river, and it is covered from light rains. The daily boat show is not as spectacular as the one you can watch every night from Rotary Park, but they do have to go out into the river sometime, so you can see a boat parade like the one in the next sketch almost any night.

Elaine and Jim Hummel

And the sunsets! Step out in front of the pavilion pillars and you have nearly a full 180 degree panorama of the river in front of Clayton. No better spot exists to be ready to grab a shot of one of the most spectacular sunsets in the U.S. In the bench picture below there is one building on the western horizon, behind the group in chat formation. That is the Calumet water tower, which is lit at night.Over the 19 years since, Carol and I have been regulars at the benches, now primarily at Frink Park, and look forward to greeting all the other regulars each summer.

From lower left, clockwise: Carol Charles, Al Thompson, Sandy Thompson, Grace DeBoer, Bud DeBoer, Bernie Miller, Margie Miller, & a gentleman I can't identify.

We missed the 2008 season due to astronomic gas prices, and we sold our trailer home in 2009, but we have spent two to three weeks in rental homes since, except for the summer of 2020 because of the pandemic. In the intervening decades since 2004 we have lost some of our Bench Buddies. Bud DeBoer passed away in 2019, and Ron Houppert in 2020, and are sorely missed. Grace and Anne still join the group when they can. Anne lets us store our chairs in her garage, and as we find it harder to walk lately, lets us park in her driveway occasionally

Grace DeBoer and Anne Houppert

Alyse Ritchie, Margie Miller, Bernie Miller

You cannot do without friends. The river is a beautiful place, but without the friends, it is just a place to be.

Other Group members after dinner at the Thousand Islands Harbor Inn, before we got to Clayton in 2015. From left: Jim and Elaine Hummel, Jim and Brenda Knight, Al and Sandy Thompson, Ron and Anne

I am dedicating this chapter to all those whom we got to know in those years. May we see them again next summer. If we could afford it, we would spend the whole season, from May to October, living along the river.

Bernie Miller, Anne Houppert, Ron Houppert, Al Thompson, Sandy Thompson. Notice the absence of the iconic sculpture of a leaping Muskie by Will Salisbury. The River lost a great artists with Will's passing in 2022

Bernie and Margie Miller, 2022

Frink Park just at sunset, with all the folks gone home

Elaine Hummel, Jim Hummel, Joel Charles, Carol
Charles, Anne Houppert, Ed Chesko,
Grace DeBoer, Anna VanTassel, Alyse Ritchie.

Carol and Joel Charles in front of the Scoop. iPencil painting on
iPad (Below) Clayton 1000 Islands Marina, iPad painting

The marina is on The River Walk in front of the Thousand
Islands Harbor Hotel from Frink Park.

And last, one of my favorite (if not one of my best) iPencil paintings, of my friend Bernie Miller and me headed out from the dock in his boat, passing the House Boat Duchess at the Antique Boat Museum. We were on our way to fish for perch off Bartlett Point. On another trip Bernie took me for a boat ride down to Alex Bay and back. On the way home from the Bay he let me drive the boat up Millionaire's Row, all the way back to French Creek Bay. He even let me stop and take photos of Rock Island Light, a subject I have drawn and painted many times. It was the first time I'd been able to drive a boat since 2004.

Bernie and Joel, goin' fishin'. Houseboat La Duchesse in the background. Grayscale print of digital painting from photo by Margie Miller

Bernie and Margie are good friends to us, and to many others in the area, and of course, two of the Bench Buddies.

Once again, my apologies if I've left anyone out or repeated myself. I've tried to include photos of everyone, but the older I get, the smaller the Central Processing capacity gets. Until next summer, may you all have the best of times possible. We hope to see sunset on the river again. Perhaps we'll see you too! I hope you've enjoyed my trip through memory lane in art, and that you will decide to visit this wonderful place sometime soon.

****

If you live there, or visit often, or have visited Clayton in the past, I hope I haven't made too many factual errors. If you found this book interesting. Please recommend it to friends, and please visit me on Facebook if you like. I have my own page under Joel Charles, and two Clayton pages. The latter are:

Clayton, NY Fans - Commercial and Clayton, NY Fans.

If you care to look at the rest of my art, most of it is located on Fine Art America at: https://joel-charles.pixels.com/

ACKNOWLEDGEMENT

To my wife Carol, my patient and consistent reader and editor, Rebecca Kinnie of the Little Book Store in Clayton for spending the time to educate a novice self publisher, and Kathy Danielson for the friendship she has shown for a novice artist. Without them and their encouragement I doubt this book would have happened.

ABOUT THE AUTHOR

Joel Charles

 Born in Plattsburgh, NY, Joel grew up in Clayton, NY, and graduated from Clayton Central School abd Syracuse University. He has been a 10th Grade English teacher, an insurance adjuster and agent. He was honorably discharged from the U. S Army after six years of reserve service. Active in Boy Scouting for 25 years, and Rotary for 20 years.,Joel holds the BSA Silver Beaver award, and the Rotary Paul Harris Fellow award. Married to Carol Ticknor for 57 years, they have two children and five grandchildren. After retiring Joel took up acting, directing, painting and building sets for several theater companies in his eighteen years in Tucson, Arizona. He is an artist, and a published author. He previously ghost wrote four novellas, wrote and published a novel, an autobiographical series of essays about growing up on the river and many articles for the Thousand Islands Sun.

BOOKS BY THIS AUTHOR

Get Off My Butte

Science Fiction. Retired from the miliary, "Tree" Birchard finds a job that is completely in line with his military experience, and far more rewarding. And dangerous.A highly secret agency is trying to save the entire galaxy, but only one planet at a time

Pk, Growing Up Tame: Thousand Islands Memories

A collection of stories and photos from the author's life on the St. Lawrence River, a wonderful place to grow up, live and visit.